Primary health care reviews

GUIDELINES AND METHODS

Primary health care reviews

GUIDELINES AND METHODS

A. El Bindari-Hammad

Adviser on Health and Development Policies
Office of the Director-General,
World Health Organization,
Geneva, Switzerland

D. L. Smith

Public Health Physician
Pakistan Child Survival Project
Management Sciences for Health
Islamabad, Pakistan

World Health Organization
Geneva 1992

WHO Library Cataloguing in Publication Data

El Bindari-Hammad, A.
    Primary health care reviews: guidelines and methods/
    A. El Bindari-Hammad, D. L. Smith.

    1.Data collection — methods   2.Primary health care — organization
    & administration   3.Primary health care — standards   4.Quality
    assurance, Health care   I.Smith, D. L. II.Title

    ISBN 92 4 154437 6   (NLM Classification: WA 540.1)

TYPESET IN INDIA
PRINTED IN ENGLAND
91/8816-Macmillan/Clays-7500

Contents

Preface

Since 1978, when the global primary health care initiative was launched, there have been various efforts to strengthen information support for monitoring and evaluating progress. The most prominent of these is the WHO Common Framework for Monitoring of Health-for-All Strategies, which has been used in two triennial cycles, in 47 countries, as a basis for reviewing and reporting on progress in implementing the health-for-all strategy.

At the same time, WHO has developed a number of approaches for the monitoring and evaluation of specific programmes, such as those dealing with immunization, water supply and sanitation, drug supply, and the control of diarrhoeal diseases. These methodologies are being used in a growing number of countries.

The approach described in this publication began in 1982 as an effort to develop a broad-based methodology for use by countries for both assessment and planning, to enable them to diagnose their own situation and to plan for the future. It includes sets of possible indicators that cover policy and strategy implementation as well as management, effectiveness, and quality of specific programmes. It also looks at community utilization, satisfaction, coverage, and involvement with priority health activities and decisions.

Primary health care reviews provide an overview of both strategic and operational issues, with emphasis on strengthening programme implementation and decision-making at national, provincial, and district levels. They can also indicate the areas that require further research or in-depth study and analysis. Finally, they provide very useful operational information for countries wishing to monitor their progress using the WHO Common Framework for Monitoring of Health-for-All Strategies.

The methodology for primary health care reviews has been developed from the start in a spirit of close collaboration among many WHO programmes, representing both health infrastructure and science and technology. An initial version, based on experience in several national reviews, was made widely available in 1984. The present version draws on additional experience with over 40 national primary health care reviews and, in particular, the suggestions of participants in a series of reviews in the WHO African Region.

These experiences emphasized the wide diversity in the primary health care situation in different countries, and the importance of carefully adapting the review methodology to the priorities and programmes in each particular setting. Consequently, the present guidelines include sets of key issues and questions to be raised during the planning of a primary health care review, rather than the questionnaire format used in the experimental version. It is hoped that this approach will facilitate the adaptation of the materials for use in a wide variety of situations. Specific questionnaires are proposed for certain areas where experience has shown that the formulation of appropriate questions is particularly difficult. More detailed questionnaires are included for use at the community and household levels.

It is hoped that the guidelines provided in this book will prove useful to those in countries, provinces, and districts who are interested in monitoring and evaluating national progress in implementing primary health care. Any comments or feedback based on experiences in adapting and using these materials will be a most welcome contribution to the further improvement of the methodology, and should be sent to: Division of Strengthening of Health Services, World Health Organization, 1211 Geneva 27, Switzerland.

Acknowledgements

An endeavour such as this draws heavily upon the knowledge, skills, experience, and goodwill of countless persons. It is not possible to express in words our appreciation of the important contributions of the hundreds of people at all levels of both national and international health systems who have participated in various stages of national primary health care reviews. The contributions of the participants at the two workshops on Primary Health Care Reviews in The Gambia and Swaziland in 1985 had a major influence on the approach taken in the present publication.

A number of people have made substantial contributions to the evolution of the present version. These include: Dr Ben Akim, formerly WHO Representative, The Gambia; Professor John Bennett, formerly WHO Staff Member assigned to the UNICEF Regional Office for Eastern and Southern Africa, Nairobi, Kenya; Dr H. A. B. N'jie, Director of Medical Services, Medical and Health Department, Banjul, The Gambia; Dr José Rigau, formerly Field Services Division, Centers for Disease Control, Atlanta, GA, USA; Dr Somsak Chunharas, Office for Technical Cooperation and Health Manpower Development, Ministry of Public Health, Bangkok, Thailand; Dr Mel Thorne, Department of International Health, School of Hygiene and Public Health, Johns Hopkins University, Baltimore, MD, USA; and Dr Ronald Waldman, formerly of the International Health Program Office, Centers for Disease Control, Atlanta, GA, USA.

Annex 1, concerning sampling methodology, was prepared by Dr A. J. Woods and Dr Steven Bennett, Statistical Services Centre, University of Reading, England. It is based on a series of discussions in WHO, Geneva, involving staff from the Divisions of Diarrhoeal Diseases Control, Family Health, Epidemiological Surveillance and Health Situation and Trend Assessment, and Strengthening of Health Services. This group was concerned with the adaptation of the cluster sampling method used by the Expanded Programme on Immunization to broader use for sampling households rather than only children of a particular target age group. The assistance of Dr Woods and Dr Bennett in developing practical solutions to field challenges, without losing sight of statistical considerations, was of great help to the group in formulating the sampling and analytical options presented here.

Within WHO, the development of the primary health care review methodology has run concurrently with the efforts of a number of programmes to develop more detailed programme-specific modules; the review methods of the Action Programme on Essential Drugs, Diarrhoeal Diseases Control, the Division of Environmental Health, the Expanded Programme on Immunization, the Division of Development of Human Resources for Health, and Maternal and Child Health have been most useful inputs to our work. The interest and cooperation of staff from these programmes, as well as from numerous other programmes including Control of Acute Respiratory Infections, the Division of Communicable Diseases, Health-for-All Strategy Coordination, the Division of Epidemiological Surveillance and Health Situation and Trend Assessment, Malaria Control, Nutrition, Schistosomiasis Control, and Tuberculosis have been generous and very helpful.

Two persons have contributed greatly to the final technical preparation of the text, as well as to other aspects of methodological development. These are Dr Henriette Jansen, formerly Associate Professional Officer, Division of Strengthening of Health Services, and Dr Jack Woodall, Division of Epidemiological Surveillance and Health Situation and Trend Assessment.

The task of typing and retyping a series of revisions during the course of preparation has fallen heavily on a number of shoulders. Particular gratitude is due to Ms Janet Habgood and Ms Paula Bevin for their generous and cheerful assistance.

Introduction

The commitment of a country to implement primary health care (PHC) for its citizens carries a parallel responsibility to monitor its implementation. Many methods can be used for such monitoring, including analysis of existing records, case studies, and surveys. In this manual, several approaches are combined into a single exercise aimed at providing a comprehensive analysis of a national primary health care programme. Much of the data to be reviewed could be collected through the country's routine health information system, and would be available for systematic review on a regular basis. However, information support systems for the management of the health sector are not yet fully operational in most countries and, where they do exist, they are frequently under-used. This manual, therefore, includes guidelines for carrying out a PHC programme review based not only on the analysis of existing health information, but also on complementary information obtained by means of a population-based survey.

> A PHC review is not meant to be a substitute for the development of a routine health information system in a country. On the contrary, it should both stimulate and supplement the development of such a system.

PHC reviews will be useful not only to countries with explicit national policies on PHC, but also to countries trying to develop such policies. The World Health Organization has supported, and will continue to support, Member States in the planning and execution of PHC reviews and subsequent assessments. Collaboration may be provided through technical cooperation among developing countries, for example, by bringing in representatives from countries where reviews have taken place. It must be emphasized that a PHC review is undertaken in the interest, and for the benefit, of the individual country concerned.

The present publication is a guide to conducting a PHC review that can be adapted to the needs of individual countries. The process of adaptation, although frequently discussed, is often not taken seriously enough. The primary purpose of the review is to provide countries with the information that they themselves need, and, thus, international standardization of study design is not necessary.

For this reason, great emphasis is placed on the planning phase of a PHC review. Any action resulting from the review process should be based on objective, reliable information. This publication, therefore, includes guidance on existing information that might be collected and analysed and the kind of complementary new information that might be useful for arriving at a plan of action for the future. Methods and sample questionnaires for obtaining the suggested information are discussed.

It is strongly recommended that the suggestions made in this publication should be carefully reviewed and adapted by the national authorities responsible for conducting a PHC review.

Major activities

A PHC review involves an appraisal of the policies of a country regarding PHC, an analysis of specific strategies for implementing these policies, and field visits to ascertain the extent to which the policy implementation strategy has been translated into action throughout the country. The review comprises four major activities:

- the retrieval and review of existing information;

- the collection of new information;

- an analysis of all the collected data, and the preparation of a report;

- a meeting with high-level policy-makers to consider the results of the review and to develop a plan of action.

Aspects to be covered

Ideally, a PHC review should cover the aspects of primary health care outlined below.

1. *Health aspects*
The health aspects involve an evaluation of the process, output and impact of the PHC programme from the health sector perspective, using various indicators that reflect the results in terms of health

sector performance, health activities output with respect to individual programmes, and the health impact.

2. *Social aspects*

The social aspects involve an evaluation of community involvement in health, including the influence of people at all levels in bringing about better health, the outcome in terms of community satisfaction, and human resource development at the community level.

3. *Intersectoral aspects*

The third dimension is an evaluation of the intersectoral aspects of the PHC programme. This includes an assessment of how the contributions of other sectors, such as agriculture and education, are affecting the health of the people. Different sectors may have certain policies and activities that affect people's health, either in a positive or a negative manner, though there may not be explicit health objectives in these policies and activities. Thus, it is crucial to examine this particular aspect and to determine how better collaboration between sectors could be achieved, in order to bring about an improvement in the health of the people, or at least to minimize, or compensate for, the hazardous health effects of particular activities. Conversely, it is necessary to assess the effect that health development itself has on other developmental sectors.

While some countries may choose to conduct a PHC review mainly as an evaluation of individual programmes proceeding from the centre (central government or national level) to the periphery (community level), taking into consideration the social dimension of the programmes, others may prefer to review the intersectoral dimension of PHC as well, in order to bring about more concerted efforts towards PHC.

Objectives of a review

The level of detail of each review of the different dimensions of PHC and its specific components and programmes will vary according to their stage of development.

> The main objective of a review is to identify the strengths and weaknesses of a national programme, in order to establish or adjust priorities and to make specific recommendations for future action.

However, even without complete analysis of every dimension, the PHC review should be able to identify areas requiring further evaluation. Since the review is intended to assist the officials concerned (including those in sectors other than health) to formulate or modify national policies and strategies within the context of primary health care, another measure of its success will be the extent to which it is able to influence national decision-makers and development planners to make objective decisions about the future of developmental activities.

In this sense, the review should be seen as a tool to be used both to measure and to effect change, and not as an academic exercise in collecting information for its own sake.

In most countries, the review process will be conducted by a team including national officials from the ministry of health and other ministries whose activities are associated with health sector concerns (e.g., agriculture, water resources, commerce, education). The team might also include representatives of international agencies and donor countries that support PHC activities, nongovernmental organizations (NGOs), and senior health managers from other countries.

Benefits of a review

The primary health care review itself can be beneficial in many ways:

- It provides an occasion for much of the health information in a country to be collected and analysed. In this way it can serve to strengthen the national surveillance system or routine health information system.
- It provides key decision-makers with an opportunity to be directly exposed to the situation in the field.
- It promotes contact between health workers at all levels, so that views can be exchanged and a better understanding of the obstacles confronting each kind of worker can be gained.
- It gives the various sectors a chance to look at their contribution to the health of the people, in the hope that this will lead to more cooperative action in the future.
- It provides a venue for discussion between national authorities and international organizations, donor countries, and NGOs with the result that cooperation can be enhanced, and duplication of effort perhaps avoided in the future.
- Finally, the fact that the PHC review involves leaders and workers at all levels constitutes a powerful force for undertaking necessary changes.

PART 1

Manual of procedures

Introduction

Logically, the PHC review can be divided into three phases: planning, data collection,[a] and synthesis. The components of each phase are presented and discussed in this section.

Although the most visible and active part of a PHC review consists of 3–4 weeks of intensive team effort during the data collection phase in the field, the total activities involved in the preparation and conducting of a review require 3–6 months. Organization, planning, preparation, and careful coordination need to be given serious attention. The benefits to be derived from the review are proportional to the thoroughness with which the planning activities have been carried out.

---

[a] In these guidelines, the phase of the review during which data are collected in the field will be referred to as the "survey" phase.

1. Planning procedures

Planning is probably the most important phase of the review, since it will determine the quality of the work that will lead to the formulation of recommendations by the review team and, subsequently, the modification of policies and strategies by national decision-makers. Planning has to be carried out at both the administrative and technical levels, as described below.

Administrative planning

The decision to undertake the review

Previous PHC reviews have been found to be useful because they have provided an opportunity:

- to measure the progress made in the implementation of PHC, in terms of the extent to which targets for coverage, use, and impact of health services have been defined and achieved;

- to identify obstacles to continued progress;

- to identify the extent of progress of the different elements of PHC;

- to validate existing data regarding PHC implementation in the country;

- to gather data not routinely collected, especially data regarding the process of PHC programme implementation;

- for high-level programme managers to conduct field visits and to review many policy questions with local staff;

- for high-level decision-makers to come together and make plans based on new data that they have assisted in collecting.

It is important that the decision to undertake a review be taken by officials at the highest level in the ministry of health (i.e., the minister or the director-general for health). These officials, and similarly high-placed officials in other agencies, should also identify the key issues that they feel should be addressed in the review, the type of information that they expect to receive, and the ways in which it will be used to improve the implementation of PHC.

Reviews are costly, not only in terms of direct expenditure but also in terms of the diversion of manpower from other tasks. Therefore, it is important that they be undertaken at an appropriate time, with a clearly stated purpose that is understood by all concerned. National officials should determine the appropriate time to conduct a review, according to earlier programme plans calling for a review at a specific time, or according to the judgement of programme officials. If PHC component programmes, such as the Expanded Programme on Immunization (EPI) or Control of Diarrhoeal Diseases (CDD), have been the subject of recent reviews, these should be taken into consideration. Many countries find that it is more cost-effective to perform an overall PHC review rather than reviews of individual programmes.

Assignment of responsibility for the review

In order to maximize the impact and value of a PHC review, it is essential to assign clear responsibility for the review to a review team comprising designated individuals from appropriate ministries. The team should be made up of a team leader, a national steering committee, and a technical committee.

In most cases, the task of coordinating the review will fall primarily on the team leader, who should be a senior official, intimately involved in primary health care, with a personal interest in the assignment. His or her responsibility to those requesting the review must be clear. This person should be temporarily relieved of all other duties, and should be provided with adequate political and administrative (including clerical) support.

The steering committee should be charged with overseeing the conduct of the review. In many countries, there is already a national committee for PHC. Such a committee, if it exists, may be the logical body to act as the steering committee, particularly if it already has experience in tackling PHC issues through intersectoral collaboration. The steering committee should be composed of decision-makers from various sectors and representatives of the different levels of the health system, including the community. This committee should set the schedule for the review, appoint a technical committee, select participants, arrange financing, and provide periodic guidance.

The technical committee should be assigned responsibility for the collection of existing data, the design and implementation of the survey, and the analysis of the field data. In addition, it should be responsible for overseeing special in-depth studies, including policy and resource analyses. These should be completed prior to the field

9

Table 1. Composition and duties of the review team

Persons involved	Tasks
Team leader	
Senior official (from ministry of health)	Full-time coordination of the review
Steering committee	
Decision-makers from various sectors and representatives of various levels, including the community	Overall direction of the conduct of the review: — setting the schedule — appointing technical committee — selecting participants — arranging financing — providing periodic guidance
Technical committee	
National officials from ministry of health and other ministries and possibly representatives from international agencies, donor countries, NGOs, and neighbouring countries	— Collection of existing data (responsibility of one person or a subcommittee) — Design of survey (often with assistance from an epidemiologist/ statistician) — Implementation of survey in the field[a] — Analysis of field data — Writing of (preliminary) report (report will usually be finalized by the national officials after the rest of the team has left)

[a] Most members of the technical committee will be involved in the survey teams, acting as interviewers at central and intermediate levels and as trainers/supervisors of interviewers at peripheral (community and household) levels. Interviewers in the survey teams working at peripheral levels will often be selected from intermediate levels (e.g., district or health centre staff).

stage of the review, in order to provide the team with a better understanding of the adequacy or inadequacy of present policy and resource options.

The composition and duties of the review team are summarized in Table 1.

Formation of the review team

One of the early administrative tasks is to determine the composition of the review team. The team should be large enough to be able to supervise adequately, and complete, all planned review activities, including administrative and clerical work as well as the field work, but should not be so large that the reporting responsibilities become unwieldy. The team should consist of different categories of personnel responsible for health and other relevant sectors. There should be a balance between policy-makers, administrators, technical experts and health care providers from the central down to the community level. Members could be drawn from among the following groups (this list is neither complete nor mandatory):

- Central level:
  - planners and policy-makers
  - programme directors
  - administrators
  - health economists
  - epidemiologists/statisticians
  - trainers
- District level:
  - medical directors
  - programme managers
- Other sectors, ministries, and agencies involved in health-related activities: agriculture, education, planning, community development, communications, water resources, commerce, local government
- National NGOs: mass organizations, political parties, professional groups, voluntary agencies (Red Cross, Red Crescent, etc.), universities, health training institutions
- Donor agencies, international organizations.

One factor that has contributed to the success of previous reviews has been the diversity of expertise within the review team. The participation of organizations other than the ministry of health is more likely to be fruitful if they are invited as early as possible. Potential members include other ministries with activities affecting health, international agencies, donor countries, and NGOs that play a role in primary health care in the country. Their participation will ensure the comprehensiveness of the review as well as helping to ensure commitment for any further action that might be needed on their part. These groups should be informed of the intention to carry out the review, its purpose, the procedures involved, and the extent to which their participation is solicited. It is best to outline the scope of work for each member and to secure a firm commitment as early as possible, in order to avoid problems. Very early notification is especially necessary if funding is being requested.

The senior and most responsible programme managers from different national programmes involved in various aspects of PHC should be recruited from the beginning and be kept actively involved throughout the process, from the design of the review, through the conduct of the field surveys and analysis of data, to the writing of the report. If these tasks are delegated to less senior people, or to student or junior investigators, a major part of the value of the PHC review will be lost. Participating staff must understand the importance of being committed to this responsibility and to completing the project by a specific date.

Establishment of a timetable

Because of the cooperative nature of the review, it is essential that a schedule be fixed early. Travel plans and accommodation arrangements need to be made well in advance and logistic considerations require early attention. In setting the dates for the review, the following facts should be taken into account:

- The collection of existing information and preparation of materials necessary for the survey may require several months, particularly if special studies are needed.

- Field work may be difficult or impossible during the rainy season or periods of peak agricultural activity.

- Holidays, conferences, and the internal schedules of other agencies and organizations may cause problems that will need to be resolved early.

An important date is that of the post-review meeting at which the findings of the review will be considered by high-level officials, who will make decisions on whether to reconsider policy and modify the plan for PHC implementation (see page 32). This meeting should involve officials who participate in decision-making and will have direct control over the implementation of the recommendations emerging from the review. Officials who are expected to participate in the post-review meeting need to devote an adequate amount of time to this activity, and should be given the exact dates well in advance. It is important to make sure that most, if not all, of the officials who participate in the planning of the PHC review also participate in the post-review meeting.

A time schedule should also allow the entire team to set its own pace of work, within the confines of specific deadlines. Once the

Table 2. A sample Gantt chart for setting the schedule for various tasks

Time allotment

Task	Weeks						
	1	2	3	4	5	6	7
1		————————					
2			————————				
3				————————————			

Personnel allotment

Task	Team members	Administrative assistants	Interviewers
1	1	0	0
2	0	1	0
3	8	1	12

steering committee responsible for the review can see how events will unfold, it will be able to calculate the necessary resources (financial, personnel, time). It should be noted that some administrative arrangements cannot be made until after the sampling schedule has been designed (see pages 22–25). A Gantt chart, as outlined in Table 2, may be useful.

National and international financial support

PHC reviews are expensive undertakings. Those conducted to date have cost between US$5000 and US$30 000, excluding the air fares and salaries of team members provided by international agencies. Countries should mobilize resources, in order to be self-reliant in carrying out PHC reviews. Although, ideally, programme review and evaluation costs should be included as part of the operating budget of any programme, it is frequently necessary to seek additional funds from external sources. A comprehensive budget should be prepared as early as possible if external funding is being sought. Most donor agencies have to go through cumbersome bureaucratic procedures before funds can be obtained. It may be necessary to estimate needs early on, and hope that adjustments can be made at a later date. A possible line-item budget form is presented in Table 3.

Table 3. Example of a budget framework for a PHC programme review

	Proposed source of funds	Total for category

1. Preparatory phase
   1.1 Review team meeting:
      conference facilities
      participants
      travel costs
      secretarial support
      stationery/miscellaneous supplies
      others
   1.2 Field testing of methodology/survey forms:
      participants
      travel costs
      stationery/printing forms
   1.3 Duplication/distribution of background document
   1.4 Other expenses

2. Survey
   2.1 Survey team meeting:
      conference facilities
      participants
      internal travel to/from meeting
      hospitality/miscellaneous
   2.2 Field survey:
      daily allowance
      internal travel
      rental of vehicles
      petrol, oil, lubricants, maintenance, repairs
      drivers, guides, interpreters
      other
   2.3 Stationery and administrative costs
      Compilation/distribution of draft report
      Secretarial support

3. Post-review meeting
      Conference facilities
      Participants' daily allowance
      Travel costs
      Secretarial support
      Stationery/miscellaneous supplies
      Hospitality
      Others

Table 3 (contd)

	Proposed source of funds	Total for category
4. Publication of final report		
Compilation		
Translation		
Editing		
Printing		
Distribution		
5. Other		
Total		

Additional contributions from bilateral/multilateral agencies:		
Agency	Consultants (person/weeks)	Funded by
1.		
2.		
3.		
4.		

Logistic arrangements for central and field work

It will be necessary to arrange all the logistic aspects of both the central and field work in advance, including:[a]

- hotel bookings, both central and in the field;

- vehicle reservations, including petrol and drivers;

- in-country airline reservations, if needed;

- hiring of translators/interpreters, guides, chauffeurs, and other ancillary personnel, as required (consult work plan);

- preparation of briefing materials, field protocols, analysis forms, etc.;

- transport and per diem allowance for the field survey.

At this stage, the field survey should be announced. The support of all central offices, regions, and appropriate hospitals, districts, and villages should be solicited. They should be informed of the survey dates ahead of time.

---

[a] The number of staff needed, the time to be spent, and the logistic arrangements for the field work will be determined mainly by the sampling scheme (pages 22–25) and the survey questionnaires (pages 25–26).

Survey team

The members of the survey team should be carefully chosen. A common practice is for the members of each team to cover a variety of disciplines and personnel categories. Interviews will be carried out at different levels (households, health centres, district health services, etc.), and the choice of personnel in each team and their backgrounds should reflect this. The number of clusters that can be covered by each team is another factor to be taken into account. Not all review team members need to participate in the field stage of the survey, but one of the most welcome secondary benefits of previous reviews has been the contact promoted between central level officials, peripheral staff, and community members.

The members of the review team participating in the survey might be assigned the following responsibilities:

- to train interviewers;

- to develop a plan for reaching and surveying all randomly chosen clusters in the time allocated for this activity;

- to supervise the interviewers in order to ensure that the data being gathered are not only quantitatively sufficient, but also of reliable quality; this point cannot be overemphasized;

- to verify and tabulate the data from their area of responsibility;

- to prepare an interim report, based on a preliminary analysis of the data, to be presented to the officials in the areas containing the selected clusters and to the review team as a whole.

In general, the interviewers assigned to each survey team should speak the local language and be familiar with local customs. They should also be literate and acceptable to the local people.

If possible, experienced interviewers should be used, preferably ones with health survey experience. If it is necessary to use staff of the ministry of health, it is preferable for the staff to conduct interviews in a district other than their own, in order to avoid conscious or unconscious bias.

Training and working facilities

In addition to arranging the logistic aspects of the survey (page 15), it is necessary to arrange facilities for training and for the survey teams to do their "office" work (data tabulation, analysis, and report writ-

---

Table 4. Example of checklist of equipment and supplies for survey teams

---

1. Data collection forms:
   — household
   — health worker
   — village leader
   — health centre
   — district office
   — special purpose (water/sanitation, service records, height/weight)
2. Instruction sheets (interviewer manual)
3. Summary (tallying) forms
4. Clipboards
5. Stationery (pens, pencils, folders, graph paper)
6. Calculators
7. Maps
8. List of clusters, villages (with population data)
9. List of officials, health facilities, health workers to be met
10. Reference tables (e.g., height/weight)
11. Thermometers for measuring refrigerator temperature
12. Packets of oral rehydration salts
13. Immunization/weight cards
14. Health education material
15. Health centre/health worker drug list
16. Petty cash (funds for incidental expenses)
17. Schedule, team/vehicle/driver assignments
18. Medical kits

---

ing). The team will need facilities at both the central and provincial levels.

Supplies and equipment

All supplies and equipment should be to hand at an early date. If funds are needed for their purchase, an adequate budget should be drawn up well in advance, as discussed on pages 13–15. A sample list of equipment and supplies for survey teams is provided in Table 4, but this will need to be modified for each review.

Technical planning

Review and analysis of current policies and plans

A great deal of information needs to be assembled prior to the field-work phase of a PHC review. The first step is to collect written material pertaining to the national plans and policies for PHC as well as related development policies, e.g., policies concerning food pricing, education, and social welfare. A review and analysis of these documents should help to define the objectives and targets according to which progress in PHC implementation will be assessed. It also provides a picture of the potential contribution of other sectors to the implementation of PHC. Examples of potentially important documents are:

● national policy statements regarding PHC;

● national policy and strategies in related development fields;[a]

● national plans, including stated objectives, strategies, and targets, for each PHC component, e.g., EPI, CDD, maternal and child health (MCH);

● reports of previous reviews of PHC or its separate components, especially any recommendations made;

● plans, including stated objectives, strategies, and targets for health-related programmes and activities of other relevant sectors.[a]

This type of information is particularly important for two reasons: it furnishes the starting-point for subsequent activities and it provides the basis for an analysis of the extent to which the country has acted on its commitment to PHC. With regard to the latter, information is needed on:

● the mechanisms and procedures for coordinating the activities of all sectors contributing to health development in the context of PHC;

● the mechanisms proposed and acted on to strengthen community involvement in PHC;

● the nature of the planning process, especially any changes facilitating PHC development (e.g., change from a "top down" to a more decentralized approach);

● progress in the delegation of authority and responsibility to the peripheral levels of the PHC structure;

---

[a] The review team should have a good idea in advance which health-related policies and plans (either positive or negative) should be considered, rather than going through all national development policies and plans.

- progress in the shift of resources from urban to rural health facilities or from institutional to community-based activities (e.g., changes in the distribution of expenditure on hospitals, health centres, doctors, nurses).

If the kind of information referred to in this section is not available to the review team, it might be worth while appointing subcommittees to prepare the documents that are deemed necessary. In other words, in-depth policy and resource analysis should be undertaken prior to the field-work phase of the review. For example, studies of the effects of existing policies on the distribution of health resources by district or region, or on health differentials between different socioeconomic groups or geographical areas, should be undertaken, if this information is not available. Similarly, special studies may be needed to assess the role of private and nongovernmental agencies in the financing and provision of health services, in order to compare various financing options. If the review can stimulate national policy-making of this kind, it will have served a very important purpose.

Review and analysis of existing information

Part 2 of these guidelines describes the process for collecting existing national data. It will be necessary to adapt the suggestions presented to the needs of each country. However, in all countries, the contents of the review should be based on existing data and *ad hoc* studies.

Some PHC component programmes may have made little progress in spite of having ambitious objectives and targets, as well as an important investment of resources, and may benefit from an evaluation at this time. Other programmes may not have received the resources that were initially allocated to them, and an analysis of the reasons for this might be very useful. It might also be helpful to make a complete evaluation of PHC components that have been relatively successful over the past few years, in order to identify the elements that are necessary for the success of a national PHC strategy. Unless a complete review of existing data is conducted, it will be difficult to know how to focus the field surveys.

Extensive—probably excessive—amounts of data have been collected in past PHC reviews, much of which were of limited quality and some never fully analysed or used. Thus, early in the planning phase, the minimum information required should be specified, so that a tightly focused data collection and review process can be designed. Specific indicators should be identified before the phase of data collection, and decisions made on how they should be used in the analysis. This focused issue-identification process can help to ensure appropriate participation by team members, and that reasonable sampling strategies are designed for the field work.

The only way to determine the necessary content of the PHC survey is to review existing data. The sources of the data may vary, but one important source will be the routine health information system in the country. If the rates of incidence, prevalence, and mortality are not routinely calculated, they can be established by applying incoming reports of morbidity and mortality to calculated target population denominators. Other indicators, such as vaccination coverage, consumption of medicaments, or case–fatality rates of certain priority diseases can also be helpful in determining the focus of the survey. For example, management information regarding the distribution of personnel, budgetary allocations, and drug delivery systems will also be useful. If there are difficulties in getting the necessary minimum information through the routine national surveillance system, other sources can be explored, such as specific PHC component programme surveys (vaccination coverage, diarrhoeal disease incidence and mortality, nutrition surveys, etc.), university theses on subjects related to the national programme (these are frequently a neglected source of useful information), applied research projects, and NGO project records. It is important to stress that information used in the review should not be limited to that collected or assembled by the review team, but should also include any special expertise or studies related to the issues being addressed by the review.

The individuals responsible for compiling and analysing this information will need the cooperation of all divisions within the ministry of health responsible for collecting data and of colleagues in other ministries concerned with activities affecting the health of the people. They should have easy access to documents. This step will be the longest and most complicated, but possibly the most important, of the planning activities that precede the arrival of the full review team, especially as far as the multisectoral inputs are concerned. It may be useful to appoint an assistant for this stage and it is at this point that the technical committee (if one has been appointed) should become fully involved. As stated earlier, technical committee members should be drawn from different disciplines, and each should be able to contribute existing data from his or her division, department, or agency to the review process.

Establishment of specific objectives

All dimensions and components of PHC should be addressed during the initial review process using existing data, but subsequent detailed examination should be limited to the specific dimension or elements of PHC that are ready for evaluation. For example, if, on the basis of existing data, a country identifies a need to ascertain the causes of an apparent failure in the delivery system for drugs, it may be necessary to ask many in-depth questions at all drug-distribution centres. However, if it is not known whether drug distribution is, in fact, a serious problem, it may be sufficient to review the availability of drugs at the health-post level only.

Another way to structure the review is to identify important public health measurements (criteria or indicators, such as infant mortality, mortality from malaria, etc.), agree on a process to decide which of these indicators should be investigated in the PHC review, and then make a detailed study of the pertinent administrative and scientific issues. If, for example, mortality from malaria is one of the selected issues, then drug delivery systems would need to be examined in detail. It should be borne in mind that mortality data cannot be obtained from the survey questionnaires, and that they will have to be obtained from centrally available data.

Once the existing data have been evaluated and initial discussions have been held with top-level ministry officials, it should be possible to form a precise idea of what the review process can and should accomplish. It may be primarily an exercise dealing with policy analysis and development, a data-based technical review to monitor programme advances, an outcome-oriented comprehensive evaluation of one or more PHC component programmes, or a combination of these. Once the scope of work for the review has been established, specific objectives should be laid down and discussed with national policy-makers, the steering committee and other team members.

Additional information required

When the objectives of the review have been defined, and the existing information has been collected and analysed, the real design work begins with identification of the type of additional information to be gathered during the review. This step cannot be conducted in a cursory manner; the information needed must be defined exactly. As previously mentioned, specific indicators should be identified prior to the data collection phase, and decisions made on how they will be used in the analysis. The following points should be considered, within the ministry of health and other sectors, for each aspect of PHC to be reviewed:

- government policy regarding the particular aspect;

- existing plans for implementing the policy;

- available resources for carrying out these plans;

- the minimum data that need to be collected for a reliable assessment of coverage and use of health services;

- the need for an assessment of the quality of service delivery;

- whether the impact of the component on the health status of the target population is to be measured.

Levels of the health and social system from which additional data should be collected

In general, health systems are established on a hierarchical basis, the "lowest" level being the community and the "highest" the centre. In order to understand PHC and its problems fully, it is necessary to gather selected data at all levels, both inside and outside the health sector. It is the job of those planning the review to determine from which levels, and to what extent, additional information is needed in order to arrive at informed conclusions regarding the functioning of PHC.

One level of inquiry outside the health system must receive special attention—the household level. The individual household is the unit on which PHC is usually centred. It is only at this level that the use and impact of health and other services (e.g., nutrition, education, credit schemes) can be accurately determined. Household characteristics are strongly influenced by village or community factors. The survey should be designed to address the issue of equity in the allocation of resources to communities with different geographical, structural, or racial characteristics.

The sampling scheme

Cluster samples

The two-stage cluster-sample survey method popularized by EPI has been used in previous PHC reviews (see Annex 1). It was designed to measure immunization coverage and the incidence of, and mortality from, diarrhoeal diseases. Caution must be used when this survey method is applied to measurements or questions for which it was not originally intended. Details of alternative sampling procedures are provided in Annex 1.

Decisions about choosing a sample of households or individuals from which data are to be collected must be constrained by what is feasible within the time allocated and the budget available. Within these constraints, it is important to identify and define clearly the basic sampling unit, which for PHC surveys will usually be the household. The necessity for speed and economy usually rules out the selection of simple random samples of households, and some form of cluster sampling will be adopted using natural groupings of households, such as villages or communities. For reasons of cost or shortage of time, it will often be necessary to introduce other stages of sampling. For example, districts may be chosen first, then villages within districts, and finally households within villages (multistage sampling).

The methods of data collection and analysis described in Annex 1 will provide unbiased estimates of population variables. When an estimate is unbiased, it is possible to assess the degree of uncertainty in the estimated value by means of the standard error (S.E.). Roughly speaking, it is 95% certain that the true value of a population parameter will lie inside the interval:

$$(\text{estimate} - 2 \, \text{S.E.}) \text{ to } (\text{estimate} + 2 \, \text{S.E.}).$$

This interval is known as the 95% confidence interval.

The precision of estimates made from the survey will depend on the size of the sample, the amount of clustering, and the item for which the value is being estimated. All other things being equal, the larger the sample, the more precise any estimate will be (in other words, the smaller the S.E.). However, for the same total sample size, a survey of a large number of clusters with few households in each will give more precise results than a survey of a smaller number of clusters each with a larger number of households.

For example, a survey in which 300 mothers are interviewed will usually give more precise estimates than one in which 200 mothers are interviewed. Furthermore, if the 300 are distributed as 50 clusters of 6 mothers, the estimates will be more precise than if they were distributed as 30 clusters of 10.

On the other hand, a larger sample size and more clusters (even if somewhat smaller) will lead to an increased workload, which in turn means increased costs and time. As the resources available for a PHC review will be strictly limited, total sample size is usually a few hundred, spread over some tens of clusters. It is most convenient to pick a cluster size that can be covered in half a day or one full day's work.

Sometimes, the sample sizes required for different items in the same survey may differ greatly. For example, a survey on immunization may require a sample size of 200 children aged 12–23 months (or 800 households), whereas a survey on diarrhoea morbidity may require a sample size of 1500 children aged 0–2 years (or 3000 households) to get results of comparable precision. In this case, the larger value of 3000 for the overall sample size would be taken to satisfy both criteria. However, this would mean that about four times as much information would be collected as was needed for the question on immunization. If sufficient resources were available, this would not be a problem, as it would give a more precise estimate, but, in practice, it may be more sensible to take a subsample for the immunization question. In other words, only every fourth child, aged 12–23 months, found in the survey would be included in the sample. This would save time and effort, but would necessitate more complex instructions for the interviewers, and so should be used with caution.

Stratified samples

Suppose that a country is divided into a small number of regions—on an administrative or ecological basis, for example. Then a stratified sample can be obtained by selecting samples independently from each of the regions. The size and structure of the samples should be decided separately for each region and may vary. Each stratum should be considered as a separate survey and the precision calculated for that region. The precision of the overall national estimate will then be somewhat better than that for any single region.

Stratified samples can be obtained even when only some of the regions in the country are chosen. This will occur when regions are selected purposively. In this case, the survey cannot be representative of the country as a whole. However, it can be considered that the regions actually chosen are the "country" of interest in the survey and that the sample is a stratified sample of this "country" to which the results can be generalized.

While it is important to take care over the size and structure of the sample, it is equally important to keep in mind the goals of a PHC review; statistical considerations should not be allowed to override them. The prime consideration at all times is whether the data to be collected using a particular sampling scheme will be useful. That in turn has to be measured against the goals of the data collection, and the resources and options available. It will rarely be a question of one method being completely "correct" while another is completely "wrong". It is more likely to be a choice between the more and the less efficient, and sometimes between doing something not very well or doing nothing at all.

The following are final considerations related to sampling:

- The selection of the sampling scheme is a prerequisite for determining the personnel needed for the field-work phase, during which enough staff must be on hand to complete the work within the designated time. Estimates of staff required can be made only when the number of sites to be visited and their relative accessibility are known. Only after the sampling scheme has been defined and the staff needs determined can transportation requirements and budgetary needs be fixed.

- Before any data are collected, it is important to be sure that they can be analysed in accordance with the purpose of the survey and using the chosen sampling scheme. At this early stage (before data collection begins), some thought should also be devoted to methods of data presentation, such as the tables and graphs that will be needed.

Designing the survey questionnaires

At this stage, the nature of the survey should be precisely defined by specifying the additional data to be collected. The team should probably include at least one individual with technical expertise in the area of survey design and analysis.

For a PHC review, it is necessary to balance the breadth of each questionnaire against the depth, the desire for quantitative data analysis against the need for general policy analysis, and the flexibility afforded by open-ended and opinion-type questions against the clarity and simplicity of more structured, closed questions. In most instances, the final survey questionnaire will reflect a combination of all these concerns.

All the questions in the questionnaires need to be unambiguous and worded in a way that the respondent can understand (taking into consideration the different types of respondents to be interviewed at different levels). The household-level survey should be composed primarily of questions to which simple answers (e.g., yes or no) can be given.

The design of methods and formats for data collection will be facilitated if there is a clear idea, in advance, of how the data will be presented in the review report. Dummy summary tables should be constructed before the questionnaire is designed (see Table 5). Analysis is facilitated if the questionnaires are designed in sections covering particular programmes, which can be separated and analysed in parallel. Each section of an individual questionnaire must then carry the same identification code.

Table 5. Presentation of survey findings

A. Immunization coverage indicators according to province

Province	n_1[a]	DPT 1[b](%)	Polio 3[c](%)	n_2[d]	TT 2[e](%)
A	450	82	34	180	8.6
B	438	76	30	176	10.3
C	462	68	28	206	15.2
D	502	53	18	219	8.1
E	488	61	23	231	11.8
F	523	43	17	244	6.7
G	556	34	12	281	7.5

[a] n_1 = no. of children of target age.
[b] DPT1 = diphtheria-pertussis-tetanus vaccine, first dose.
[c] Polio 3 = poliomyelitis vaccine, third dose.
[d] n_2 = no. of women who had given birth in past 12 months.
[e] TT2 = tetanus toxoid, second dose.
Note: For data as important as this, it may be desirable to show the 95% confidence limits of the sample in the table itself, i.e., 82 ± 6.5%, 15.2 ± 4.6%, etc. If so, the data should be shown in two tables, one for DPT 1 and polio 3, and one for TT2, in order to avoid overcrowding the table.

B. Programmes represented in health centres

Province[a]	% of health centres with programmes on:				
	Nutrition	Family planning	Maternal and child health	Diarrhoeal diseases	Immunization
A	100	97	83	93	100
B	97	86	93	83	97
C	93	100	88	6	93
D	97	83	78	79	81
E	88	71	73	63	81
F	86	93	37	53	77
G	55	34	52	68	75

[a] 30 health centres per province.

Field testing of survey questionnaires

The field testing of survey questionnaires is essential, even if the questionnaires have been used before. Such testing should be carried out some weeks before the field teams are trained, and should aim to:

(a) confirm the suitability of the package of survey questionnaires, paying particular attention to clarity and the time required to complete the data collection;

(b) confirm the feasibility of using the entire package of questionnaires in a given geographical area;

(c) determine whether materials to be used in the community (the forms for the community health worker, traditional birth attendants, local leaders, and households) need to be translated into a local language to ensure standardization.

The purpose of the field test is to uncover and correct flaws in the questionnaires, in order to ensure that the data collected are reliable and accurate. The data summary forms for field analysis of survey data should also be tested at this point.

Training of the survey teams

As already discussed, the survey team should include both senior officials from the ministries involved and local people with a knowledge of the areas being surveyed. The people who will administer the questionnaires will have to be trained in both general interview techniques and the use of the specific questionnaires. Each question needs to be reviewed for clarity, to make sure that the answers obtained will be reliable, will provide the desired information, and will mean the same thing to all of the interviewers and interviewees. Special emphasis needs to be given to the questionnaires to be used at the household level, since at this level, large numbers of interviews will be carried out for the purposes of statistical analysis. Ideally, a manual (or at least a set of instructions) should be given to the interviewers together with the questionnaires. The manual could be developed during the pretesting of the questionnaires and should explain how each question should be asked, i.e., the wording to be used, whether answers should be prompted or not, whether alternative answers should be read out by the interviewer, whether only one or more than one answer can be ticked, the nature of possible alternative answers and how the questionnaires should be completed accordingly, etc. It should be borne in mind that, if more than one type of questionnaire is being used at the household level (see pages 22–25), additional instructions will be needed.

Training of interviewers should take place immediately before the field survey. It should include at least the following aspects: extensive familiarization with the manual and questionnaires by means of group discussions, role-playing and field experience with the materials, followed by discussions of errors noted during training and clarification of misunderstandings. Whenever interviewers have not been involved in earlier stages of the review (probably only those who will carry out the survey at the lower levels of the health system), they should also be told the objectives of the review, as well as the national PHC policy, plans, and strategies, in order to enable them to see the survey in context and to understand their responsibilities, and to motivate them for their assignment in this important exercise.

2. Field data collection

The field-work phase is intended to be a short, but intensive, part of the review, implemented by all or part of the review team. It consists of the steps described below.

Site visits and surveys at provincial, district, and community levels

In past reviews, the effectiveness of the data collection activity during the site visit has depended on:

- The ability of each survey team to collect reliable and consistent data—this necessitates a full understanding of individual and group responsibilities, as well as familiarity with the question-naires.

- A detailed schedule for each day's activities, not only for the interviewers, but also for the supervisors. This is particularly important at the household level, as interviewers should visit homes at times when interruption of the daily routine of the family will be minimal and, of course, when the parents are at home. The best times, i.e., early in the morning or in the evening, are often not the most convenient for members of the survey team.

- The provision of some type of service (for example, distribution of antimalarial drugs or packets of oral rehydration salts, providing that these are normally available at health posts or centres) as part of the survey effort. These activities can demonstrate, both to the community and to the participating local health workers, the proper method for performing such tasks. In this way, the survey is used as a training device.

The importance of strict supervision cannot be overemphasized. Supervisors should spend most of their time in the field. Helpful activities include:

- re-surveying a random sample of households (or health workers, etc.) and cross-checking the results against those of the original interviewers;

- collecting corroborative data wherever possible (e.g., checking for the presence of a BCG scar to confirm a child's immunization history);

- tallying the data in the field in the presence of the interviewer, in order to identify doubtful results while they can still be corrected, and to avoid repeating the mistake the next day.

Preliminary data analysis in the field

As mentioned above, the work of each team should be reviewed by the supervisor at the end of each day. This includes tallying the results for each cluster (each form should contain a section for tallying results). The preliminary data analysis consists of summarizing (in most cases, totalling) the responses to each question on a cluster by cluster basis, for example, the total number of mothers who answered "yes" to the question "Does your child have a growth chart?" If the "running totals" are maintained in the field on a daily basis, it will be quite easy to derive survey-wide totals when the teams return from the field.

3. Synthesis of data

Introduction

Once collected, the data must be organized in preparation for an in-depth analysis. On the basis of the analysis, a preliminary report should be prepared followed by a full report of the review procedures, findings, and conclusions, including recommendations for modifications to the national primary health care plan (as well as the plans of related sectors) and their implementation. The last stage in the review process is for national policy-makers to elaborate a detailed plan of action for implementing the final recommendations of the review team.

Full analysis of existing and new data

Ideally, the analytical process will have been worked out in advance by the technical committee. Once the information to be collected is known, dummy tables and graphs can be drawn up and the appropriate data added as soon as they are assembled. This is a worthwhile, time-saving step that is highly recommended. If computers are to be used, technical personnel should be prepared to use them and should know exactly what is expected of them.

The compilation and analysis of the data should be carried out by the review team, including the senior programme officers. Their involvement ensures that they will understand and appreciate the results. Data analysis should be carried out promptly, and the results presented to the entire team in a clear and understandable fashion. With regard to the presentation of data, those analysing the data should be selective in their choice of material to be presented in the main body of the final report; it should always be judged in terms of the original objectives of the study.

Preparation of a preliminary report

A preliminary report should be prepared by the review team as quickly as possible and should include summaries of the relevant data, interpretations and findings derived from the summaries, and, most important, a list of recommendations, which should be given a prominent position at the beginning of the report. The rationale behind each recommendation should be discussed in the text, using data to support the conclusions reached. Data should be presented in clear and understandable tables and graphs. The consequences of acting on each recommendation should be presented and discussed, with an indication of their relative priorities.

Preparation of a plan of action

One of the most valuable outcomes of a review is a plan of action for implementing short-term solutions. This plan might be prepared by the technical committee or by the steering committee, if it has been active in overseeing the review, or by both. Whatever the circumstances, a post-review meeting of top-level government officials should be held to discuss and—it is to be hoped—endorse the action plan. One possible format for presenting an action plan to the participants at the post-review meeting is presented below.

Programme objective	Target	Problem	Proposed solution	Estimated resource needs	Person to take action	Date to begin/end

In setting time-frames for the implementation of recommendations, potential causes of delay, e.g., necessary changes in legislation, should be taken into account. It will be useful to set approximate deadlines, even for actions that depend on sectors other than health. Such a plan can be used, among other things, in the preparation of a 5-year health plan, in human resources planning, in developing training curricula, and in formulating proposals for external collaboration.

Presentation and discussion of initial findings and recommendations (post-review meeting)

All the findings and recommendations of the review should be presented to the appropriate decision-makers before the team is disbanded. The date for a formal meeting at which the review findings can be presented to the appropriate high-level government officials should be set during the planning phase. The recommendations and the proposed plan of action, as established by national review team members, should be presented and discussed.

Preparation and presentation of the final report

The final report can be prepared in the weeks after the field visit, and does not require the entire team to remain on site. It is important to prepare a formal report to create a record of the review, to provide a tool for those charged with implementing the recommendations of the review, and as a basis for subsequent PHC reviews. The review is not complete until the final document has been prepared and distributed to the interested parties, and one person should be assigned responsibility for seeing that this is done.

Report strategy

The aim of a PHC review is to appraise the explicit policies of a country with regard to PHC, to analyse strategies for implementing these policies, and to ascertain the extent to which the policy and strategies have been translated into action throughout the country. The report must therefore be directed first at performance, indicating clearly how national health policies and strategies are being implemented, the conditions that facilitate progress, and above all the problems of implementation. The second and even more important aim of the report must be to assess the appropriateness of the health policies and strategies in the light of what has happened in the recent past and what is likely to happen in the foreseeable future. The report must not only show the health impact of previous health developments, but also indicate possible future effects of prevailing and planned policies and resources. Therefore, it is usually preferable, from the point of view of the end users of the report, such as high-level decision-makers and programme managers, for related information from different levels of the survey to be gathered and analysed together and for the report to be organized around key issues and topics cutting across the levels.

The assessment of achievements or disappointments over the past few years should be relatively straightforward, if appropriate data have been collected, especially in such key areas as resources. To this end, those analysing the data should try to separate the important information from the trivial by considering the original objectives of the review. Only important information should normally be included in the final report. The basis for making future projections is usually not firm and some guesswork will be necessary. In this context, it would be useful to attempt to look at alternative scenarios, instead of merely projecting the prevailing trends.

The size of the PHC review report is an important consideration. Since both the complexity of the health system and the extent of the PHC review itself will vary from country to country, it is not possible to provide firm guidance on size. However, the report is primarily intended for the eyes of national decision-makers. It should therefore be concise and present its message clearly and simply; it should also be eye-catching.

A sample list of contents for a report is presented in Table 6.

Suggestions for data analysis and presentation

- Results of primary health care reviews should be presented according to both administrative level (i.e., central, provincial, district, health centre, and community), and programme area or issue (i.e., policy, planning, organization, finance, MCH, EPI, malaria control, etc.).

- Where rapid initial tabulation is of prime importance, presentation according to level may be easiest. However, it should be noted that in this case important linkages between related events within programme or management areas at different levels may be overlooked.

- Those analysing the data should be selective in their choice of material to be presented in the main body of the final report. Data must always be judged in terms of the original objectives of the study.

- The data should be examined for results that distinguish between areas that require action and those that do not. For example, if over 90% of health centres in each province have completed their plans of action, it is quite appropriate simply to say "nearly all health centres have completed their plans of action", without presenting the individual statistics. Attention in the report can then be focused on the more discriminating indicators of how such plans are being implemented.

Table 6. Sample list of contents for a PHC review report

Executive summary (major findings and recommendations)
Section 1. Introduction
           Background
           Objectives of the review
           The review process (summary of study design and methodology)
Section 2. Findings of assessment
           Policy and strategies
                 Current policy
                 Community involvement
                 Other sectors related to health
           Resource analysis
                 Health facilities
                 Health personnel
                 Budget
           Management and support activities
                 Organization and management
                 Health information system
                 Logistics and transport
           PHC elements
                 EPI
                 CDD
                 MCH
                 Others
Section 3. Conclusions and recommendations
           Possible annexes
           1. Details of sample design and methods, including examples of each questionnaire
           2. List of places surveyed
           3. Names of survey team members and interviewers
           4. Tabulation of detailed findings of questions not presented in full in body of report
           5. Summary of standard errors of important survey estimates not included in body of report

---

- As far as possible, tables of data should follow a consistent pattern throughout the report. For example, if information is to be presented by province, provinces should always be listed in the same order, in a vertical column on the left of the table, unless there is a particular reason to present them in a different order or across the top of the table instead. Similarly, the location of information about sample size and use of absolute numbers and/or percentages should be similar in all tables, unless there are clear reasons to do otherwise.

- In the body of the report, tables should be limited in size with entries well spaced out for easy reading and interpretation. In general, they should not have more than 7 columns of data. It is often best to select only a few items of information from the questionnaire to illustrate a particular conclusion. It is never appropriate to try to include all the information collected in the survey in the body of the report. It is the responsibility of the analytical team to select only items that illustrate the most important findings of the survey. Full details can be included in annexes, if they are likely to be of interest to some readers.

- Graphs and diagrams should be used where possible to present results. Often much more information can be presented in a graph than in a table, and a graph is usually more easily understood (see Fig. 4 and 5, pages 56 and 61).

- Where only a few numbers illustrate a relevant point, these can be presented in the text, without including all the related numbers in a table. If a full set of data is needed to illustrate the point, it is better to put it in a table rather than list a long series in the text. In this case, an explanatory text should refer to the appropriate table, which should preferably be situated on the same page for easy reference. Data presented in full in the body of the report should not be duplicated in the annexes. Where more details are given in the annexes, it is useful to refer to the relevant annex in the text.

- Numbers should be presented only to the level of precision justified by their standard errors. In general, this means that percentages should normally be given to the nearest whole number, and only exceptionally—with small figures perhaps—to the nearest tenth of one percent. Standard errors should be reported to the same level of precision as the data to which they refer, i.e., to the nearest whole number for most cases.

- Standard errors need not be given for all, or even most, of the figures in the report. But they should be included for the most critical information regarding key indicators. This may be some 10–20% of the data in the body of the report.

- If there is likely to be wide interest in the detailed analysis of the household survey information, it may be useful to include summaries of the results for the main variables by cluster in an annex. In any case, some analysis of the variance among clusters could be carried out in order to determine the extent of clustering for critical indicators, and simplify the estimation of standard errors. This information can then be included in the annex with other details of sample design and methodology.

Follow-up

The steering committee and each responsible agency should be aware of the reforms identified as necessary by the review, the body to be in charge of carrying them out, and the date by which they should be achieved. One issue that should be discussed at the post-review meeting is the plan for monitoring the actions to be taken on the recommendations of the review. Such follow-up might be achieved through periodic meetings of the participants in the post-review meeting, or of the steering committee, to review progress. Programme officers in areas affected by the plan should be asked to respond to the recommendations. The routine health information (surveillance) system could be improved and used to monitor regularly the parameters collected during the review.

The executive summary of the PHC review should be widely distributed, especially to the places included in the survey.

The final task of the team should be to set a date for the next primary health care review.

4. Summary of PHC review sequence

Planning

A. Administrative	B. Technical
Decide to undertake review Assign responsibility for review Identify participating agencies Establish a preliminary timetable Secure financial support	Review current PHC policies and plans
Form review team	— Review existing information — Establish detailed review objectives — Determine additional information needed
Make logistic arrangements to initiate work of review team	— Specify levels of the health and social systems from which data will be collected — Design sampling procedure — Design survey questionnaires and method of analysis
Make logistic arrangements for data collection; announce the field survey Assign staff to survey teams Arrange training and work facilities	— Field test questionnaires
Procure supplies and equipment Assign analytical and reporting tasks; decide on contents of preliminary and final reports	— Train survey teams

Field data collection

Make field visits, including supervision for quality assurance
Perform preliminary data analysis in the field

Synthesis of data

Analyse data
Prepare preliminary report, including data summaries, findings, and recommendations, and indication of unpublished or unanalysed data available from the survey
Formulate plan of action for solutions
Present preliminary report to policy-makers (post-review meeting)
Prepare final report
Follow-up:
— distribute executive summary, especially to places surveyed;
— monitor actions taken on recommendations;
— set date for next PHC review.

PART 2

National level

Introduction

At the national level, the work for a PHC review involves the collection and review of existing data prior to the collection of field data. In order to complete the preparatory phase of this review, two kinds of information should be collected, analysed, and summarized. The first is quantitative data, the treatment of which involves, for the most part, displaying available figures in tables and graphs. These data are well suited to statistical treatment and can be easily communicated. However, quantitative data may not be available to answer all the questions that a review should raise, and even those available may not be of good quality.

In order to probe problems regarding the planning and implementation of health programmes, it is frequently necessary to interview the people who are most familiar with the situation. The subjective (qualitative) data obtained from these individuals may be more difficult to analyse, but in many situations there is no alternative. Conducting interviews properly, in order to obtain the desired information, is an art. A great deal of thought should be given to the questions to be asked, the order in which they will be asked, and the way in which each question will be framed. Because quantitative and subjective data will be collected from various sources, it is essential to indicate the source of each piece of information. Furthermore, the original documents from which the data have been abstracted should be available for review when the entire team is assembled.

If a PHC component programme, such as the Expanded Programme on Immunization (EPI), has recently been the subject of a separate evaluation, it is not necessary to include it in detail in the PHC review. Instead, the recommendations from the evaluation should be reviewed and comments made regarding the extent to which the recommendations have been implemented. If some or all of the recommendations have not been implemented, the reasons should be discussed and suggestions made as to whether or not the recommendations should be modified.

This part of the review is essentially the responsibility of the individuals who are organizing the review and should be completed prior to assembling the team. For a complete review of primary health care activities in a country, a great deal of information must be collected and considered. It is essential that enough time is allowed for this task. It is equally important that at least one person is assigned on a full-time basis to do the work. The output of this phase is a report, based on the information available, on the state of the national primary health care system, and a series of recommendations on the specific issues on which the data collection in the field should focus. It would be entirely appropriate, in welcoming the team members, to present at least the major findings of this report, which would serve to define the scope of work for the rest of the review process.

1. Background information

Background information is needed to guide the team members, and the other persons involved, who might not be familiar with the sociodemographic and administrative characteristics and the essential health indicators of the country. The outcome of any previous PHC review should also be thoroughly reviewed.

In order to determine trends and changes, annual data collected over a period of several years, if available, should be tabulated. Graphic presentation of trends is always useful, and several indicators can be included in the same graph. However, it is advisable to keep graphs simple so that they can be easily interpreted. The sources of all the data should be indicated.

Regional and subregional data, if available, are more useful than national figures, since the purpose is to identify potentially underserved populations.

Administrative and health divisions

Administrative and health divisions should be provided with maps of the country. The geographical areas to be reviewed should be indicated.

Population

A table should be prepared showing the size of the national population and selected segments of the population. A population pyramid may be useful to illustrate age and sex distributions (see Fig. 1). Regional populations should be described, and it may also be necessary to indicate district populations. The levels of the health system (e.g., region, district) chosen for comparison in the review will also determine the divisions for which population data will be required. Population data are usually readily available within the country from the ministries of health and planning, from the census bureau, or from the central statistics bureau.

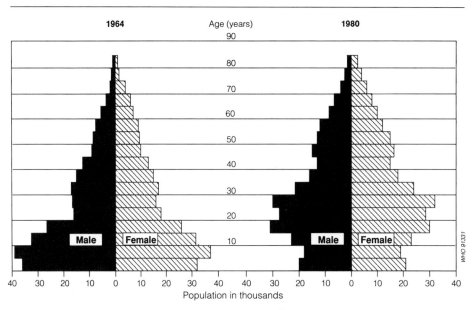

Fig. 1. Examples of population pyramids (Shanghai County, China)

From: Xu Su-En. Health statistics of the People's Republic of China. In: Halstead, S.B. et al., ed., *Good health at low cost.*
New York, Rockefeller Foundation, 1985.

Health indicators

It is desirable to use health indicators that have been chosen for the national health-for-all strategy, if they are available. However, other indicators can also be used as deemed appropriate (see Table 7). Efforts should always be made to collect data in such a way that trends and regional values are presented (Table 8). The reasons for any regional differences in health parameters should be investigated in the review.

If there is a marked difference in, for example, infant mortality rate (IMR) between urban and rural areas, this should be examined and the reasons discussed.

Recommendations of previous PHC reviews

If a PHC review has been carried out previously, a brief report of the major recommendations should be provided. The report should indicate the recommendations that have been followed and those that have not. It might also be useful to review these with the team involved in the earlier review and to have a brainstorming session on the recommendations, especially to find out whether and why they were or were not feasible. This will prevent the present review team

Table 7. Examples of national health indicators (19.. to 19..)

Indicator	19..	19..	19..	19..	19..
Crude birth rate					
Crude death rate					
Infant mortality rate (under 1 year)					
Child mortality rate (1–4 years)					
Maternal mortality rate					
Literacy rate male					
female					

Table 8. Dummy table for comparison of regional/district health indicators

Region or district	Crude birth rate (CBR)		Crude death rate (CDR)		Infant mortality rate (IMR)	
	Urban	Rural	Urban	Rural	Urban	Rural
A						
B						
C						
D						
etc.						

from repeating the same recommendations without a thorough knowledge of their feasibility.

Milestones in PHC implementation

In order to complete the background information for the review, it will be useful to illustrate some of the milestones that have been achieved in the development of the national PHC system. Examples of such milestones are: formation of a national health council or similar body; formation of an intersectoral PHC coordinating body; sensitization of parliamentarians; changes in structure of ministry of health headquarters; decentralization; policy pronouncements; changes in legislation; changes in the medical student curriculum; changes in the student nurse basic training curriculum; and establishment of new cadres of health workers (e.g., supervisors of community health workers).

2. Health policy, organization, and resources

It is essential for the team to assess the appropriateness of the policies and the adequacy of both the organization and the resources with which the national PHC strategies are being implemented. It is also important to try to identify any managerial inconsistencies and bottlenecks that tend to hinder PHC implementation. The main sources of information for this purpose will be the decision-making health officials, e.g., permanent secretary, chief medical officer, and their equivalents in the ministries of education, agriculture, planning, finance, and other relevant sectors. The team will obtain this information mainly through interviews and review of documents.

National health policy

An attempt should be made to define the policy context within which the entire PHC review will be conducted. Issues to be raised include whether there is a national body for health policy formulation and who the members are (give names and/or designations), and the nature of the main factors that have been considered in formulating health policies, e.g., epidemiological factors, subpopulations at risk, existing inequities in health service accessibility.

The team should also discover whether there is a document or legislation spelling out policy directives and whether there is a stated policy on the following questions:

- equity in health care (universal access according to need);

- coverage by health services;

- prevention of disease and promotion of good health;

- intersectoral activities in relation to health;

- decentralization;

- strengthening of the health infrastructure;

- community involvement.

Contributions to health from other sectors and agencies

The policies and programmes of certain key sectors, such as agriculture, education, information, water, public works, etc., which are part of the national development plan, can have a great impact on the health of the people. These policies may not have any specific health objectives, but nevertheless produce an impact on health that is sometimes even more significant than the health sector's contribution. Examples include national strategies to combat poverty, emphasis on industrialization and urbanization, improvement of female literacy, rural job creation, and food pricing policy. These programmes are clearly the responsibility of sectors other than health, but unavoidably affect health in either a positive or a negative way.

It is suggested that the following questions should be asked to obtain core information from all relevant sectors. Note also the name and the function of the person responding.

- Are you aware of the national goal of health for all by the year 2000? If so, what is your sector's contribution towards the achievement of this goal, e.g., specific programmes developed (describe what they are and for whom) or reorientation/strengthening of the health component of existing programmes? If not, does your sector contribute (or know of a contribution that it could make) towards improving the health status of the population? (If so, specify.)

- Do you consider the health aspects of the programmes of your sector during the planning phase? (If so, give an example.) Do you request technical advice on the health implications of your programmes during this planning phase? Have you received the technical help requested? If so, could you give some concrete examples, including from whom you received technical help?

- If you did (or do) not seek advice from the ministry of health, why not? (Reasons might include, for example, that the person believes there are no health implications in the programmes/projects, or that the ministry of health should be brought in only when health-specific problems arise.)

- Do you have any suggestions for establishing or improving links with the ministry of health? If so, how, in which areas, and during which phase of your sector's planning? Do you believe the ministry of health can contribute to your sector's objectives and programmes? (If so, specify.)

Additional specific questions in relation to health should be formulated for the various sectors, and visits to these sectors should be

49

arranged to obtain the answers. The answers must be sought from policy-makers in the respective ministry (director-general, under-secretary, etc.). Examples of issues that might be raised are given below.

Ministry of education

In general, the education sector can have health objectives in the following four areas: (*a*) the teaching of health as a subject in schools; (*b*) the delivery of health services in schools, e.g., subsidized meals; (*c*) the school serving as an example of a healthy environment (water, sanitation); (*d*) paying special attention to vulnerable groups by promoting female literacy, girls' attendance, etc.

To analyse the role of the education sector, you might wish to use some of the following questions:

- Do you have specific health information/education in the school curricula? Are the topics related to the priority health problems of the country? (If so, specify.) Did the ministry of health provide you with the technical information required to develop the health education component in your curricula? Is there a programme for training teachers in health education?

- What standards for environmental health measures are provided in your schools, e.g., for the supply of safe water and latrines? What measures related to the health services do you provide in your schools, e.g., immunization, school meals, growth monitoring, family life/sex education, first-aid training and kits, sport/physical training, periodic health examinations, screening for disability, and integration of the handicapped? Are there norms and standards for all the above? Have these norms been developed by: the ministry of education alone, the ministry of education in collaboration with the ministry of health, or the ministry of health alone?

- Do schoolchildren participate in health activities in their communities? (If so, give a concrete example.) Do you have a policy and a programme for promotion of female literacy? Does it have a health education component? (If so, specify.)

Ministry of agriculture

The agriculture sector can also have both positive and negative health impacts. For example, it might provide work, income, and nutritious food, all of which are positive; negative impacts might result from irrigation projects, the use of pesticides, or programmes that are not aimed at reducing inequities. The following are some examples of questions that might be asked:

- Is malnutrition a priority problem in the country? If so, which groups are most affected, and where are they located? Does your sector carry out specific activities to solve this problem? (If so, specify.) Do you have any specific activities with health targets? (If so, specify.) Are these activities carried out by the ministry of agriculture alone? If not, which other ministry or sector collaborates and in which activities?

- Do you have an intersectoral mechanism with respect to food and nutrition that brings together key sectors involved with the ministry of agriculture? (If so, describe members or committees to whom they report, and the matters with which they deal.)

- Do you train field workers in nutrition? (If so, describe their activities.) What is your policy for crop promotion—cash crops or food crops? Is there a food pricing policy? (If so, specify.) Is there a programme to promote the use of pesticides? If so, how is it controlled? Have irrigation schemes been developed for certain parts of the country? If so, how has the health impact been dealt with?

Ministries dealing with industry, housing, and the environment

The sector dealing with the environment serves as another important example to be considered in the review. Some of the questions that could be asked of a policy-maker from the ministry concerned are:

- Is there any legislation regarding industries that cause environmental pollution? (If so, specify.) Is a surveillance system available for environmental pollution? (If so specify.) Is there any policy regarding health care for workers in industry? (If so, specify.) Is there a special housing programme for the poor, particularly in the urban areas? Is there a programme to provide financial subsidies or loans for community activities to improve housing? Do you and the ministry of health consult with each other on the above activities? Do you collaborate with other sectors on the above activities? If so, with whom and how?

Ministry of information

If it were to use its potential effectively, the information sector could play a very powerful role in tackling the health problems of a country. In order to analyse the present situation, the following are some of the questions that might be asked:

- What are the major health problems in the country? Who are the most affected, e.g., age group, geographical area, urban/rural? What is the source of this information? Have you developed any programmes to inform the public of these problems and to develop greater awareness? If so, can you give specific examples of the programmes developed, the media used, and the target population reached? Do you have regular media programmes on health issues? If so, which issues were dealt with during the last 6 months? How often? Who provides you with technical guidance on the health information that you diffuse, e.g., ministry of health, universities, research institutions, NGOs, others? What are your suggestions for increasing public awareness of health problems and their prevention?

The next thing to be assessed is whether any mechanism exists at the central level whereby health aspects can be brought to the attention of different sectors, when they are formulating their policies and plans. For example, is there any mechanism for the joint formulation of national policies and plans? Which sectors, NGOs, and voluntary agencies are involved? How often are they supposed to meet and how often do they meet? Have they been considering health aspects in the formulation of their policies and plans, or is there an intersectoral coordinating mechanism specifically for health development? Are there permanent coordinating bodies at the regional, district, or community level?

Community involvement

An attempt should be made to determine the extent to which central level tries to involve the community in PHC policy formulation and programme implementation. What policies and strategies for community involvement in health planning, if any, have been formulated in the national system of government? To what extent, and by which processes, are community priorities reflected in national programmes? Can the community influence the formulation of PHC policies through its members of parliament, the mass media, or specific associations?

What has been done to strengthen such arrangements and opportunities in order to increase the community's voice in health affairs? What training has the ministry of health given to its personnel to prepare them for work with communities? Information about these aspects should be obtainable through discussion with senior health officials and other officers in the central offices of the other ministries.

Organizational structure

The structure of the ministry of health should be assessed to determine the extent to which it facilitates implementation of PHC. This includes looking at the management structures at the central level and tracing their linkages within and outside the health system. To this end, the team should examine an organizational chart of the ministry of health, including the central level structures. This chart should be attached to the report. (Fig. 2 and 3 are examples of charts of a department of health and a comprehensive health system, respectively.)

Are the roles and responsibilities at central and district levels adequately defined? Is there adequate decentralization? Are there adequate mechanisms at appropriate levels for the coordination of

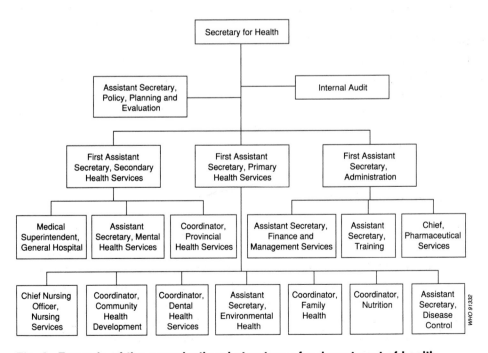

Fig. 2. Example of the organizational structure of a department of health

53

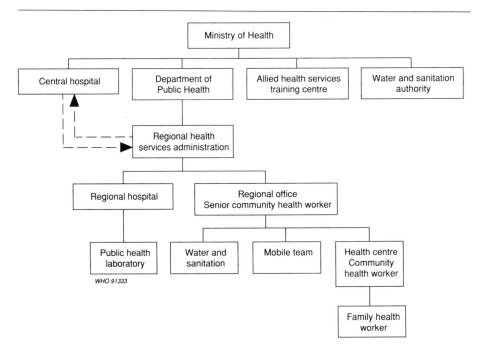

Fig. 3. Example of the organizational structure of a comprehensive health system

technical support for PHC? Are the present procedures for communicating policy decisions to managers at the regional and peripheral levels satisfactory? (Specify problems and indicate solutions.) What organizational changes should be introduced into existing structures in order to improve managerial effectiveness and efficiency?

Budget and financing

The team should examine available information on recurrent and capital health expenditures, in order to determine the trend in national health budget levels in relation to other national expenditures, and to establish whether there is a shift in the distribution of national health finances towards supporting PHC strategies. The percentage of the national budget allocated to health is a good indicator of national commitment to PHC, especially if health resources are redistributed in favour of the underserved (see Table 9). An attempt should be made to find out whether existing funds have been reallocated in favour of PHC, particularly for vulnerable groups. The team should inquire

Table 9. Dummy table to show national budget allocations and expenditures over past five years

Ministry	19.. Est. %	19.. Act. %	19.. Est. %	19.. Act. %	19.. Est. %	19.. Act. %	19.. Est. %	19.. Act. %	19.. Est. %	19.. Act. %
Health										
Education										
Defence										
Agriculture										
Water										
Information										
etc.										
Total national budget										

Est. = Approved estimates.
Act. = Actual expenditure.
% = Column as % of total national expenditure.

about measures being taken to increase efficiency in the management of available health finances.

Most of the required information can be found in the national treasury, the national annual budget estimates, or the accounts division of the ministry of health. If data covering a number of years are available, it will be useful to present them graphically, in order, for example, to depict the trend in the health budget levels in relation to the national budget and those of other sectors, or the trend in how the health budget is divided according to level of service or geographical division. Table 10 and Fig. 4 illustrate how such data might be presented.

Recurrent expenditure pattern

What proportion of the health budget is allocated to staff salaries, in comparison with funds reserved for the purchase of goods and services to enable such staff to do their work effectively? Does the budget indicate equitable distribution and adequate attention to priority PHC programmes? A map showing per capita expenditure on health in each region is a powerful way of pointing out inequitable distribution of resources. Budgetary data can be tabulated to show regional and/or district distribution (see Table 11), as well as allocation according to programme (e.g., MCH, nutrition) or according to level of service (e.g., national or teaching hospitals, regional hospitals, basic health services).

Table 10. Dummy table to show trends in per capita health expenditure over the past five years

	19..	19..	19..	19..	19..
National health allocation per capita					
% annual inflation					

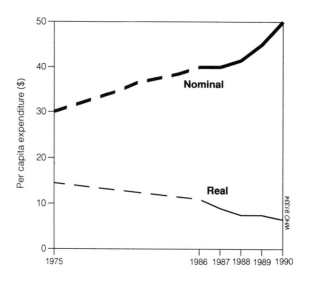

Fig. 4. Per capita annual health expenditure

The team should take a close look at who prepares the budget, who has the authority to transfer funds from one item to another, who is responsible for the disbursement of funds, and who is authorized to solicit and receive money directly from donors. This information has to be broken down according to level of service (permanent secretary, director of medical services, hospital authorities, regional and district authorities, etc.). What is the government policy on the mobilization of community resources for health? Is a fee-for-service or cost-recovery scheme in operation in the country? (If so, describe). Have there been

Table 11. Dummy table to show regional health expenditure per capita over the past five years

Region	19..	19..	19..	19..	19..	% change 19.. to 19..
A						
B						
C						
D						
etc.						
National						

Note: The team can use this type of table to assess equality in the distribution of budgetary finance, but should take into account variation in need, if data on the distribution of health problems are available.

any local studies on ability to pay? If so, what were the findings and how have they been used?

Development and external resources

Most developing countries receive aid for health development in the form of external grants and loans. However, these funds are rarely fully reflected in the financial statements of ministries of health. As a consequence, external contributions may not be effectively applied to the national health planning process. Furthermore, the approach of certain external health assistance tends to divert scarce national resources (manpower, time, and counterpart funds) away from the national priorities.

The PHC review may be an opportunity not only to update data on resources obtained from the ministries of finance and planning, or from the local offices of multilateral and bilateral agencies and NGOs, but also to remind all concerned about the need for integrated national health planning. A significant part of external resources may be provided in kind (drugs, vehicles, fellowships, technical assistance, etc.), or for specific projects. Every effort should be made to quantify all such assistance in order to facilitate planning. Where there is a significant contribution to health care delivery from the private sector, an effort should be made to obtain data on this also (see Table 12).

Table 12. Dummy table to show external contributions to the health sector, 19. . (*This table is partly filled in, to give an example of the nature of the information to be collected*)

Donor agency	Purpose	Area covered	Amount (in $)	Nature of assistance
1. Donor governments				
(*a*) Norway	Technical assistance	National hospital		Grant
(*b*) Sweden	Infrastructure	Rural health		Loan
(*c*)	Transport/EPI	National		Grant
(*d*)	Drugs	National		Grant
2. Multilaterals				
(*a*) WHO				
(*b*) UNICEF				
(*c*)				
3. NGOs				
(*a*) Red Cross				
(*b*) Oxfam				
(*c*)				

Health personnel

Health professionals are as important a resource as money. The team should try to determine the extent to which appropriately trained personnel are being equitably deployed. However, equity should not be measured only by normative population-to-worker ratios, but should also take into consideration variations between regions, for example, in terms of ease of travel, the dispersal of the population within the region, and the extent and nature of health problems. Information should be sought on whether there has been any systematic re-deployment of staff. Information about the past and present distribution of staff and about personnel policy and plans should be available in the ministry of health (see Tables 13–15).

The attrition rate and morale of the health staff are other aspects that should be considered in the review. As far as the attrition rate is concerned, the required data will be collected from appropriate health staff tables in the ministry of health. The following information should be ascertained. If the attrition rate is high, is this for some or all cadres? Can clear reasons be identified for the pattern? Can anything positive be done about it (see Table 16)? The interviewers of senior health officials should seek to determine whether staff motivation is given adequate attention. Are a significant number of trained health staff currently unemployed? Are trained health personnel seeking

Table 13. Dummy table to show distribution of health personnel according to region, 19. .

Region	Projected population	Doctors	Assistant medical officers	Medical assistants	Health officers	Rural medical aides	Health assistants	Nurses	MCH aides
		NO. OF OCCUPIED POSTS							
A									
B									
C									
etc.									
Totals for regions									
Voluntary agencies									
Total for country									
		PROPORTION PER 100000 POPULATION							
A									
B									
C									
etc.									
Totals for regions									
Voluntary agencies									
Total for country									

Table 14. Staffing norms for health facilities (19. .)

Staff category	District hospital	Major health centre	Minor health centre	Dispensary	Health post
Physician					
Dentist					
etc.					
Total staff					

Note: During the field survey, the team will compare the actual situation in each facility within the survey sample with the specific target for the facility, and make appropriate conclusions and recommendations.

Table 15. Dummy table to show trends in the distribution of health personnel according to level of service[a,b]

Staff category[c]	Primary level			Secondary level			Tertiary level		
	19. .	19. .	19. .	19. .	19. .	19. .	19. .	19. .	19. .
Physician									
Dentist									
Medical assistant									
Registered nurse									
Registered midwife									
Assistant nurse									
Sanitarian									
Pharmacist									
Laboratory technician									
CHW									
TBA									
etc.									

[a] The definitions of levels of service must be clearly stated for each country, if this table is to be meaningful.
[b] Show a period of at least 3 years.
[c] List in accordance with staff categories or groups prevailing in the country.

Table 16. Dummy table to show attrition rate[a] according to staff category (%) (*time period preferably 6–10 years*)

Staff category	19. .	19. .	19. .	19. .	19. .	19. .	Main reasons[b]
Physician							
Dentist							
etc.							

[a] Attrition rate to include losses during both basic training and in service.
[b] For example, salaries, housing, hours of work, marriage, pregnancy, retirement, poor promotional prospects.

employment in other fields? Are incentives provided to attract staff to "hardship" areas?

In order to facilitate the team's assessment in this area, one or more tables should be prepared depicting the main categories of national health personnel, if possible over a number of years, and subdivided according to employer, geographical division, and level of service. A table portraying staff attrition rates will also be useful. Where possible, diagrammatic or graphic presentation is even better. Examples of such presentations are given in Fig. 5 and 6.

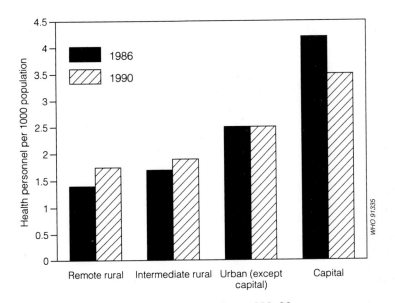

Fig. 5. Change in health personnel distribution, 1986–90

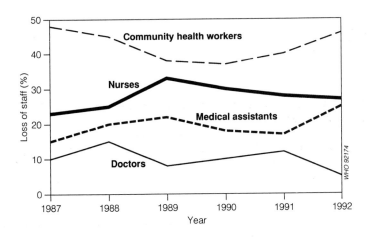

Fig. 6. Percentage of staff leaving the health service by category, 1987–92

Training

It is not sufficient merely to list the number of training courses available in the country and the numbers of participants in each course. An attempt should be made, on the one hand, to identify areas of progress and, on the other, to identify areas of deficiency or inconsistency that require corrective action.

For a full assessment, documents should be examined, central-level health managers interviewed, and some of the main national health training institutions visited. Issues in question include the following: What is the national policy on health training? Is the training capacity for each main type of worker sufficient? Have any new courses been introduced as a result of the national PHC plan? Are training curricula designed or modified to provide the specific knowledge and skills required to operate programmes? Is training output generally meeting demand and are there specific plans for future training needs? What proportion of personnel needing a specific type of training (e.g., EPI, CDD courses) has received such training? Have basic health training curricula in the country been revised or reoriented in response to PHC priorities? (If so, specify which basic curricula and the main changes made.) Are there built-in mechanisms to ensure that basic training curricula are periodically revised to respond to changing service needs? (If so, describe.) Is the ministry of health involved in the in-service training of personnel from other sectors (e.g., agriculture, education, water, community development) and vice versa? (If so, specify how and to what extent.)

Retraining of existing staff is an important aspect of the implementation of PHC strategies. The team should establish the extent of in-service training and whether it is integrated into programme management (see Table 17).

Health facilities

It is important to determine whether health facilities have been equitably distributed throughout the country, according to needs. This type of information can be obtained by examining the distribution of health facilities according to region (see Table 18). The types of facilities to be included in the tables will depend on the national situation, as will the decision to include private and NGO facilities in the same table or to present them separately. If data on the regional population are available, the population coverage of each type of health facility can be calculated. The team should establish whether

Table 17. Dummy table to show in-service training courses and participants, 19. .

Programme area	Course title	Date	Place	Number of participants	Type of personnel
EPI					
CDD					
MCH					
etc.					

Table 18. Dummy table to show regional data on health facilities

Region	Years ago	Type	Hospital		Dispensaries	Health centres	Village health posts
			Specialized	General	Urban Rural	Urban Rural	
A	10	Public					
		Private					
		Total					
	5	Public					
		Private					
		Total					
	Current	Public					
		Private					
		Total					
B	10	Public					
		Private					
		Total					
	5	Public					
		Private					
		Total					
	Current	Public					
		Private					
		Total					
Etc.							

any regions are significantly underserved and, if so, whether plans have been made to improve their coverage.

It would be most useful to present data showing changes in the number of different types of health facility per population over the past 10 years, at both national and regional levels. Using these data as a basis, the reviewers should ascertain the national policy on relative rates of growth of various levels of health facilities. For example, are available resources concentrated on tertiary and specialist facilities at the expense of other levels? Is there an explicit strategy to ensure

Table 19. Dummy table to show percentage of funds allocated to different types of health facilities according to source of financing, 19. .

Type of facility	Government	Mission/NGO	Private	Total (100%)
Specialized hospitals				
General hospitals				
Capital city				
Regional				
District				
Urban health centres				
Rural health centres				
Dispensaries				
MCH centres				
Family planning clinics				
Health posts				
Obstetric beds				
Paediatric beds				

that tertiary and specialist levels of the health system do not receive a disproportionate amount of resources? (If so, describe.) The team should carry out a resources analysis (see Table 19).

As with most of the data collected so far, this type of information is quantitative. The team must also, through interviews with appropriate officials, determine the qualitative aspects, such as the adequacy of maintenance of facilities, the adequacy and appropriateness of staffing, equipment, and medical supplies, and the quality and range of services offered. The field survey teams will, of course, inspect in greater detail the health facilities that fall within the survey sample.

Additional useful planning information includes:

- % of total population living within x (to be defined) kilometres of a functional health facility;

- % of total population with access to outreach services (define access);

- % of total population living beyond access (as defined) to functional health services.

Where no firm data are available, it would be useful to include figures based on interview data; such informed opinions should not be discounted.

3. Programme management

Another aspect to be reviewed is the adequacy and efficiency of central management of PHC components. As already mentioned, if a PHC component programme, such as the Expanded Programme on Immunization, has recently been evaluated, it is not necessary to include it in another detailed data-gathering activity. Instead, this part of the review should provide essential minimum information on important programmes and aspects of PHC in order to permit a broad assessment of the extent to which PHC in general and the individual programmes in particular have been implemented. It is up to the national authorities to decide which PHC programmes should be evaluated in detail and which should be left for other occasions. This decision will depend partly on the types of activity being carried out in the country, partly on the availability of resources, and partly on the availability of recent data.

Policy and planning

The information required should be collected from available documents and through interviews with appropriate national officers at the central level. The original documents from which the data are derived should be kept for review by the team as a whole. Data should also be obtained from interviews with programme managers.

Answers to the following questions should be obtained for each PHC programme. Is there a responsible official at central level? What are the programme's objectives and targets? Has the technology to be used been specified? Have requirements for personnel, facilities, transport, supplies, and logistics been worked out? Has a time schedule for implementation been drawn up, together with a detailed budget and a system for monitoring and evaluating the programme? What are the mechanisms for integration with the work of other programmes? A brief description of the achievements of each programme, any problems encountered, and plans for dealing with these problems, should be given.

Supervision of programmes

It is important that central managers develop and maintain supervisory contact with activities undertaken at the periphery in each programme. Information required for review of the situation may be collected by interviewing senior health officials at the central level and, if possible, examining their plans for supervision. The quality of supervisory visits should be assessed later, during the field visits to selected regional and district health facilities. An attempt should be made to determine whether the supervisory visits made by central-level staff to regions and districts have had beneficial results, either directly or indirectly. This can be deduced from the description offered by central managers on programme activities, and from what has been done to ease bottlenecks.

Programme coordination

As regards programme coordination, the following questions should be asked. How often do programme managers meet? Do they carry out joint planning? Do they discuss together the outcome of supervisory visits, and identify gaps and weaknesses? Do they plan joint action to overcome difficulties? (Give examples.)

Central management of supplies

An attempt should be made to determine whether there is an efficient system for the central management of supplies. Several factors should be considered including procurement planning and processes, storage practices, distribution efficiency, and available budget. For example, are drugs ordered in bulk using generic names, in order to obtain the most favourable prices? Are essential items given priority? Have standard lists of drugs been prepared for different levels of the health care system? Can data on the receipt, distribution, and levels of supplies in stock be easily retrieved? Have shortages of essential drugs and vaccines for programmes been anticipated in good time? Does the central warehouse provide adequate storage facilities for vaccines and other supplies?

Specific PHC elements

The team should review national policies and guidelines for specific PHC programmes. What are the main activities and targets? Is there a proper balance between programme staffing and other resources at the national level? Which manuals or modules describing how to review programme operation are being used at this level? (Examples of titles of modules are given in Parts 3 and 4 of these guidelines, and might be used by the team itself to formulate more questions.)

A basic list of key indicators for the review of specific PHC elements at national level is given below. It is recommended that inquiries should be made about the past 5 years, in order to make conclusions on trends. For each indicator, state the year to which it applies and the source.

1. (Population with safe[a] water in the home or with reasonable access/Total population) $\times 100$ = ——%

2. (Population with adequate[a] facilities for excreta disposal/Total population) $\times 100$ = ——%

3. Immunizations performed during the last 5 years (in infants and pregnant women)

Immunization	19. .	19. .	19. .	19. .	19. .	Trend[a]
BCG						
DPT1						
DPT3						
Polio 1						
Polio 3						
Measles						
Tetanus toxoid 1						
Tetanus toxoid 2						
No. of births (target population)						

[a] Conclusion on trend:
+ + = Significant increase (number of immunizations at least doubled in the last 5 years)
+ = Moderate increase (number of immunizations increased by at least 25% in the last 5 years)
0 = No increase (increase is less than 25%)
? = Unknown

4. (Population with access to local care and essential drugs/Total population) $\times 100$ = ——%

The criteria involved are:
— Availability of treatment for common diseases and injuries

[a] In accordance with national definitions.

— A regular supply of essential drugs. (Is there an uninterrupted supply of the drugs designated by the country as essential? To all parts of the country?)

— Is there a health facility within one hour's walk or travel? (If data on time taken are not available, but distance is, distance can be converted into time. For example, under many circumstances, it is possible to walk 5 km or to travel 25–50 km by motor transport in one hour, depending on road or track conditions. Conversion factors can be calculated according to terrain.)

5. Expected number of births (n) (crude birth rate × population) $= —$

6. (Number of pregnant women seen by trained personnel/n) × 100 $= —\%$
Disaggregation according to place of care and type of personnel is recommended. The average number of prenatal visits should be calculated and compared with the national norm (if there is one). The type of training of the personnel should be described.

7. (Number of deliveries attended by trained personnel/n) × 100 $= —\%$
Disaggregation according to place of delivery and type of personnel is desirable. The rate, together with the data on the place of delivery (home or institution) and type of training (nurse, midwife, CHW, TBA), should be compared with any national norms, to determine whether the situation is satisfactory.

8. (Number of infants seen by trained personnel/n) × 100 $= —\%$
The average number of infant visits/contacts and the type of care provided (including level of training of personnel) should be compared with any national norms, to determine whether the situation is satisfactory.

9. (Number of home-based records (growth chart/immunization card) distributed to infants/n) × 100 $= —\%$

10. Percentage of newborn infants with birth weight less than 2500 g $= —\%$

11. Percentage of children under 3 (or 5) years of age who are below reference value of weight-for-age $= —\%$

12. (Number of reported cases of diarrhoea in children under 5 years/Number of children under 5 years of age) × 100 = ——%

13. (Number of children under 5 years treated with oral rehydration salts (ORS)/Number of reported cases of diarrhoea in children under 5 years) × 100 = ——%

14. (Number of children under 5 years treated with home-made rehydration solutions/Number of reported cases of diarrhoea in children under 5 years) × 100 = ——%

A number of other questions that are relevant to the review of specific PHC elements are to be found on pages 70–72.

Transport

In many instances, the health sector may depend on a central government agency for the maintenance of means of transport. The team should establish whether the central-level health management has its own maintenance facilities and an explicit transport policy. The opportunity should also be taken to obtain a description of important problems and achievements in transport management.

Does the ministry of health have an explicit policy on transport management? (If so, give a brief outline.) What is the procedure for controlling the use of vehicles and preventing abuse? Are there any criteria for the allocation of available vehicles to specific services and programmes? (If so, describe.) What proportion of planned activities has been disrupted over the past 12 months, as a result of transport failure or fuel shortage?

Outreach MCH clinics	= ____%
EPI	= ____%
Supervisory visits	= ____%
Distribution of supplies	= ____%
Ambulance referrals	= ____%
etc.	= ____%

Which region was most affected? What percentage of vehicles, out of the entire fleet of reparable vehicles of the ministry of health, is currently off the road?

Health education

The aim of the evaluation in this section will be to determine whether PHC and other health activities are being adequately supported by a thriving health education service. The following information should be ascertained. Is there a national health education service? How many people are engaged full-time on health education at the national level? How many of these are trained, and at what level? Are health educators actively involved with other sectors in planning, developing, and coordinating community health education and health information activities? Is the national health education service actively involved in ensuring that health education and primary health care principles and methods are included in training programmes? Are there mechanisms for evaluating health education activities?

Does the national health education service promote, support, coordinate and/or participate in health services research? Is an identifiable amount budgeted for health education at the national level? How much of the total national health budget is allocated to health education? Is health education budgeted for by technical programmes? What is the total budget for each programme, and how much in each programme is allocated to health education? Are public information services for health available within the ministry of health, ministry of information, or other sectors? If so, list the sectors producing health education materials, and where these materials are distributed.

Monitoring and evaluation

Most PHC component programmes are subject to either continuous monitoring or periodic internal evaluations that are designed to measure progress towards the targets set at the time of programme planning. This might involve baseline surveys at the start of the programme, followed by periodic surveys of, for example, vaccination coverage, use of oral rehydration salts, availability of essential drugs, etc. The team should be brought up to date on the progress that has been documented during the course of programme implementation. In other words, this is the place to review data that have been collected for programme purposes without necessarily becoming part of national health statistics.

Where comparable data are available over time, tables or graphs could be produced to illustrate the extent and rate of programme development. For example, has there been at least a doubling of the number of immunizations given over the past 5 years? An increase of at least 25%? If there has been no increase, why not? Is it because of a change in the target age or vaccination schedule?

Trends in the number of cases and deaths due to notifiable diseases or those under surveillance should be tabulated for the past 5 years, as well as morbidity and mortality from the 10 most frequent causes, preferably analysed separately for children under 5 years and adults (15 years and over). Are surveillance data available from sentinel stations? Are data available on age and/or immunization and treatment history of cases? Is there evidence that reported incidence data are used for evaluation? Have sample surveys been conducted on any of the PHC components (e.g., immunization, diarrhoea, maternal and child health, family planning)? If so, describe action taken on the basis of the results of these surveys.

The routine reporting system can be evaluated as follows:

a. Number of reporting units (regions, provinces) = ——

b. Number of reports that should have been received in the past 12 months (if monthly reporting is required) $a \times 12$ = ——

c. Number of reports that have been received in the past 12 months from all reporting units = ——

d. Indicator of completeness of reporting $(c/b) \times 100$ = ——%

e. Number of reports received during past month = ——

f. Indicator of timely reporting $(e/a) \times 100$ = ——%

To get a picture of how the EPI programme operates, for example, the number of vaccinations given in each region should be reviewed (see pages 66–69). The size of the target population in each region should be calculated from knowledge of the population pyramid and the regional population figures. Results should be reported in terms of the number of vaccinations of each type per 100 or 1000 individuals in the target group. Comparing results will give a general indication of where the EPI is functioning best and where there are operational problems. An even more accurate measure of EPI operations, and one that, to some extent, also measures quality, breaks down vaccinations performed according to the age of the child. A high quality EPI programme will be achieving a relatively high rate of fully immunized children of less than 12 months old. If this information is available by region, some differences in quality can be detected. (Information on cold-chain integrity or vaccination techniques will not be known until on-site observations are made.) The same kind of analysis should be carried out for other component programmes under review, using appropriate indicators.

The results of monitoring and evaluation activities should be interpreted in relation to programme targets, and any recommendations resulting from these activities should be reviewed to determine the extent to which they have been acted upon. These steps should already have been taken by the programme officials who directed the surveys. When either monitoring and evaluation or follow-up of monitoring and evaluation activities has been inadequate, this should be documented by the team, and the information transmitted to the appropriate officials so that specific corrective action can be taken.

PART 3

District level

Introduction

The aim of this part of the review is to assess the effectiveness of the organization and management of PHC at the district level.[a] Emphasis should be placed on what personnel actually know and do, as opposed to what they are supposed to know or should be doing. Methods of obtaining information on national PHC policies and programmes have already been outlined in Part 2. At the district level, the same information is often requested, not to duplicate earlier information, but rather to determine the extent to which personnel at the district level are aware of and understand the policies, and to what extent they are being implemented. If, for example, as a result of its findings, the team determines that the details of national policy are not well known or poorly understood at the peripheral levels of the health system, it might recommend that a seminar be held for district and other personnel, in order to ensure that all parts of the system are working towards the same goals. In this case, it might also recommend that the system for dissemination of central policy decisions be revised or strengthened.

Another important function of this part of the review is to verify the information collected at national level. For instance, the delegation of authority may, in practice, be more limited than was planned; personnel and supplies supposed to be situated in a particular place may not be there; vehicles that have been assigned may not be functioning, and so on. There will undoubtedly be discrepancies between the information gathered at the central level and that obtained at the intermediate and peripheral levels. The team should decide how important these discrepancies are, and whether they are systematic or isolated instances. They should also determine their causes, and suggest ways in which the flow of information and communication between the various levels of the health system can be improved, if necessary.

The introduction of a new dimension in information gathering in this and the succeeding parts of these guidelines complicates data analysis. From now on, the analysis of information will have to take into consideration not only differences between levels, i.e., central versus intermediate and peripheral, but also differences within levels, i.e., between one district and another. The extent and quality of PHC

---

[a] If required, a set of questions can be developed for the regional level using material from both Part 2 (national level) and this part.

policy implementation will not be uniform throughout the country, and the review should seek to identify strong and weak areas, so that lessons learned from the former can be applied to the latter.

Finally, even more at the district level than at the central level, information obtained from discussions with health personnel and individuals from other sectors will be very important in identifying areas for priority action following the review. If there are operational difficulties and inconsistencies within the system, and if objectives and targets are not realistic, these facts will be brought to light at this and lower levels. It is difficult to quantify problems that lead to lack of motivation; these need to be discussed at length with individuals and the findings communicated to all concerned, so that the problems can be corrected. The patience and skill of team members will therefore be of paramount importance.

1. Background information

General profile of the district

The main objective of this part of the review is to determine the extent to which district officials are familiar with the geographical areas and the people for which they are responsible, and to establish a baseline against which to assess the appropriateness and effectiveness of the district health system. This information will also be useful as a reference for findings from other levels, such as the health-centre level.

Absence of knowledge or lack of easy access to this information are important findings, as such knowledge and information are basic tools for good management. To this end, district maps, if available, should be provided at the outset. The maps should clearly show the administrative subdivisions of the district and the location of health facilities, including the location of the facilities and villages that are within the survey sample.

District health officials should also highlight geographical and logistic difficulties peculiar to their part of the country, which adversely affect health service coverage, use, and management. Such problems could be that the district is too large for efficient management by the health staff provided, or that the district system of communications and transport is not adequate for health supervision and referrals. A brief outline of socioeconomic development activities within the district should be elicited from officials, in order to identify social and economic differences between various areas within the district.

Population

Health officials should be knowledgeable about the people in their area, particularly the principal target populations, such as mothers and children, the very poor, and other high-risk groups. Health officials will be unable to assess needs or service performance without knowing the size of these subpopulations. Data on other characteristics of the population, such as migration and population density, should also be collected. Estimates of the per capita income and level of literacy should be obtained, not only for the whole district but also, if possible, for smaller areas within the district.

Health indicators

For programme planning and management, district health managers should have an up-to-date idea of the basic health indicators within their area of responsibility (see Table 20). If concrete data are not available, it would still be useful to ask for approximate figures, or at least to discover whether it is felt that the rates are higher or lower than the national average. Such information should be compared with the figures available at the central level.

It is important to determine the infant mortality rate (IMR) for the district (number of deaths of infants under 1 year of age/number of live births × 1000) and to find out whether it differs significantly between males and females or from one part of the district or one particular subpopulation to another.

Table 20. Dummy table to show trends in district health indicators

	19..	19..	19..
Crude birth rate			
Natural growth rate			
Infant mortality rate (under 1 year)			
Child mortality rate (1–4 years)			
Maternal mortality rate			
Literacy rate			
—male			
—female			

2. Health policy, organization, and resources

Health policy

One important aim of this phase of the review is to determine the extent to which health managers and managers from other sectors, including political officials and others responsible for the overall administration of the district, understand and implement national health policy. To this end, the team should discuss selected aspects of the national health policies with managers at this level. For example, what are the main features of the national PHC policy? Is there a national plan to construct new health centres and dispensaries? The team should also find out if the district health office has copies of written national policies, as this may be a positive sign of good communication from the central level.

Policy formulated at the central level may not reflect the special needs of a particular district. For example, national policy may not recognize a locally important endemic disease for which a particular area may be the only focus. The team should investigate the extent to which district managers have participated in the formulation of national policies and also the extent to which national policies have been adapted to respond to district needs.

Contributions of other sectors to health

Data on the contribution of other sectors to health can be collected by reviewing documents, and noting the operational details of various programmes that have implications for health. If reports exist on the progress of implementation, they should also be reviewed. Official documents related to various intersectoral mechanisms, including minutes of meetings, are also useful in indicating how well the mechanisms have been functioning. The work of the team will be facilitated if the district health authority has already prepared the ground in advance, by gathering and reviewing relevant policy and programme documents from other sectors. During its visit to the district, the team will then be able to verify information about contributions to health. However, it will be necessary for the team to select, in advance, the information that it would like to ascertain from the documents.

views with officers of various sectors are necessary, especially
_ocuments are not readily available or are incomplete. Inter-
_ are also needed to assess the awareness, attitude, and commit-
_ _t of officers from various sectors.

Health effects of other sectors

An attempt should be made to determine the activities in other sectors
that have an impact on the health of the people. While these activities
may be implemented by individual sectors without explicit health
objectives, they may nevertheless produce positive or negative effects
on health. Examples of sectors that may be of particular interest for
the review include: education, agriculture, industry, commerce (trad-
ing), public works (including waterworks), and housing. The team
should try to find out the types of activity that are being implemented
at this level, as well as the population groups that are most affected by
them. It might also be worth while to find out whether there are
synergistic effects. The following are some specific examples of the
officials to be interviewed and questions to be asked.

The official in charge of education might be asked: What types of
services, such as school lunches, are provided in preschool facilities
and primary schools? Is there a basic educational policy with special
emphasis on female literacy? If there is a female literacy campaign,
does it focus on remote and underserved areas where the general
health status of mothers and children is poor, and does it include
health advice?

The official in charge of agriculture might be asked whether cash
crops are promoted and, if so, whether such promotion diverts resources from food production, leading to a scarcity of food among
farmers when crop prices are low, but, on the other hand, possibly
creating better food availability when crop prices increase (seasonal
variations). Other relevant issues might be whether there is a food
price policy for certain underserved groups and whether there is
promotion of nutritious crops in areas where many children are
malnourished.

The official in charge of housing might be asked whether there is a
housing policy that affects the living conditions of people. Information
could be obtained from the official in charge of water, about, for
example, irrigation schemes, which might bring about better access to
water but, if not properly managed, might also create breeding
grounds for vectors of certain diseases.

If the area under review is an industrial zone, the team might consider the possibility of paying a visit to a factory.

The following questions could also be asked for each of the different sectors. Which programmes under your responsibility have an impact on the health of the people? (Give examples.) Have you ever collaborated with health sector officials in planning their implementation? (If so, give examples.) Have you ever considered the health implications of the programmes under your responsibility? In what way? Do you have any educational activities or training to help your staff understand the relationship between their work and the health of people? If so, who organizes these activities? Are there any subpopulations that receive special attention? If so, who are they? Where are they located? How large are they?

Coordination between sectors

Besides identifying the various programmes that may affect health, and the extent to which they are being implemented, the review team must also make an effort to assess how these different programmes are coordinated to bring about better health for the people. Are they coordinated at all? Is there a mechanism by which different sectors (including NGOs and private groups) carry out joint planning of their programmes? Are the health implications of different programmes being considered by the various sectors through such a mechanism? How can health officials draw the attention of other sectors to the influence of their programmes on health?

Are there any examples where the programmes of different sectors have been formulated and implemented taking health consequences into consideration? Has there been any joint decision to implement programmes in various sectors focusing on improving the health of the underserved population? The review team should assess the awareness of officials from other sectors regarding the health implications of the programmes under their responsibility, as well as their attitude and commitment in working on an intersectoral basis to achieve better health for the people.

Community involvement

At this level, the team should look for concrete examples of community involvement in development and health. The review team should assess whether representatives of the community participate directly in the planning and implementation processes for both health and other aspects of socioeconomic development. If mechanisms for community involvement were described at the national level, are these actually in practice at the district level? Are there representatives of the community in the official district organizations for general development and health? Have the district authorities adopted any other specific measures to promote and sustain community involvement in health development, through, for example, the use of mass media, or provision of information on the local health situation and the options available for improving it? If so, by whom, when, and how are these measures implemented? The team should discuss these issues with the district administrators and health managers.

The following are some concrete examples concerned with community involvement: Are there any community groups that carry out health programmes/activities? Which ones? For example, women's groups, NGOs, religious groups, youth organizations? Give examples of what these groups do. Do district health officials consult with them? Are joint programmes being developed together with these groups? Are these programmes coordinated? By whom?

Another important aspect is the role of the community in the running of health facilities. The team should find out: (a) the relationship of the hospital administration to the community (if there is a board, whether the community sends a representative), and (b) whether resources are provided (either in cash or kind).

The team should seek out further evidence of community involvement. Important pointers would be whether any government decisions have been taken or modified as a result of community requests and action. Were these issues reported in the mass media? Does the district provide seed money to community groups as a means of encouraging them to match it with their own resources?

Organizational structure and decentralization

In assessing the organizational structure at district level, the main aspects to focus on are: (a) which organizations/institutes provide health care, and (b) how they are coordinated. The team should ask the district health managers to produce an organizational chart and, on the basis of this, discuss whether there is a district health team, how the different organizations/institutes are included in a district-wide work plan, and what are the lines of responsibility, supervision, etc.

They should then discuss any problems related to the current organizational structure of the health services, whether there has been any integration of programmes, and, if so, how this has affected them.

In discussing the organizational structure, the team should aim to establish whether there is adequate delegation of authority, as well as responsibility, from the national level. Does the district medical officer and his or her team feel hindered in the performance of duty by bureaucratic central control? What is the extent of direction from national level? Is national policy sensitive to the special needs of the district? Are the district authorities empowered to redeploy staff? The interviews should explore the extent of the power of local decision-makers, especially with regard to resource allocation (see also page 84).

The extent to which the district health organization has recently been reoriented to support PHC implementation is another aspect to consider. What administrative mechanisms or structures have been created and do they include mechanisms for consultation with colleagues from the central level and in other districts? The team should focus on the degree of autonomy that has been granted to district health staff in the management of the various PHC components. For example, are they authorized to set district targets and objectives, and to prepare and operate district PHC programmes? Is this in accordance with national policy?

Planning and management

For each PHC programme, answers should be obtained to the following questions. How is planning carried out? By whom? Is there a responsible official at district level? What are the programme's objectives and targets? Has the technology to be used been specified? Have requirements for personnel, facilities, transportation, supplies, and logistics been worked out? Has a time schedule for implementation been drawn up? Is there a detailed budget and is there a system for monitoring and evaluating the programme? A brief description of the achievements of each programme, any problems encountered, and plans for dealing with these problems, should be given (e.g., is there a system for referral of problems to the next higher level, and, if so, does it work?). What are the mechanisms for integrating with the work of other programmes? Is there a management team? If so, who is involved (health care providers, other sectors, community representatives), and what are the tasks (e.g., supervision) and work schedule?

Budgeting and financial management

This important matter is rarely given the attention it deserves. This part of the review should focus mainly on the degree of decentralization of the financial management of the health service. The sensitivity of the central planning machinery to the priority needs of various districts will be assessed by examination of differences in the allocation of funds to different programmes and different areas. It should be ascertained: whether the district health team is consulted when the district budget is being prepared; which activities receive the major share of the budgetary allocation; and whether these allocations correspond to national or district priorities. Details of such allocations should be available at national headquarters as well as in the district health administrative office. Additional insight into the degree of decentralization may be obtained by asking, for example, which of the members of the district management team hold funds for emergency purposes, and whether the district raises any resources itself (e.g., charges, taxes).

Health personnel

The aim here is to assess how personnel are distributed and whether they are being deployed according to need. The team should determine the distribution of staff according to category and facility as well as the distribution of posts and vacancies in the district. It is important to check whether the information tallies with reality, by visiting sample facilities. The team should also look for inequities in the assignment of staff to the various facilities and check whether there are any un-

Table 21. Dummy table to show number of staff assigned to health facilities

Staff category	District hospital	Health centre A	Health centre B	Health post A	Health post B	Etc.
Physician						
Nurse						
etc.						
Total staff						
Population served						

Note: During the field survey, the team will compare the actual situation in each facility within the survey sample against the specific targets for each such facility, and make appropriate conclusions and recommendations.

served areas. This information should be presented in appropriate tables (see Table 21). The team should ask whether measures have been planned or taken to cope with staffing shortages and whether any changes have been introduced in staff use and deployment as a result of starting the PHC programme. The appropriateness of staff qualifications for service in the district should also be examined.

Common problems associated with the employment and management of health personnel, especially outside the capital city, should be identified, including the conditions that affect staff morale and motivation. For example, whether there are incentives for staff working in remote areas and whether there are career structures. In order to obtain a balanced opinion on the situation concerning staff morale and other personnel problems, interviews should be carried out, not only with the head of the district health management team, but also with a cross-section of all types of personnel.

Training

An active training programme is a sign of a thriving PHC system. The following issues should be raised. Which categories of personnel are being trained? Is appropriate attention paid to all categories? Is training being carried out in teams? Which subject areas are covered? Are important topics in PHC being taught? Who plans the training and who implements it? Details of in-service training over the past year, including courses, who organized them, and for which categories of personnel, should be listed and the following information obtained. What are the important outstanding needs for in-service training? What proportion of priority target groups (e.g., nurses, midwives, or combined groups) has received such training? What factors influence the curricula of courses taught, e.g., budgetary provisions made by special programmes? The team should also establish whether the district health authorities have made adequate arrangements and have sufficient resources for training purposes. Are health training institutions operating in the district? Are district hospitals engaged in training staff? Is the training they give relevant to actual needs? Is there joint training across programmes?

Role, function, and accessibility of health facilities

The main purpose of this part of the review is to find out about underserved areas and population groups and to see if existing facilities could be more fully used. Information should be sought about the numbers, types, and distribution of private and NGO facilities in the district, and whether they are supplementing the coverage of the public sector. The following questions might also be asked: Does the district manager know the catchment area for each facility? Are the functions of each facility specified in writing? Is there coordination between the public facilities and other facilities? Are the facilities equitably distributed and appropriately located in relation to population distribution, transport, and communications? Are there adequate arrangements for referral of patients?

Does the district hospital actively support PHC programmes? Does it provide outreach and preventive services? Does it interpret the information it receives from lower levels and provide feedback? Does it monitor the quality of the care it provides?

3. Operational management of programmes

The team should look at how the various PHC components are being managed at the district level (this is also partly covered under "Organizational structure and decentralization", pages 82–83). How and by whom are they managed? Are there satisfactory arrangements for supervision, logistics, and evaluation? The review should also be directed at such important supporting activities as health education and health information. In addition, this is an opportunity to examine disease prevention and control activities in the district.

It is essential to gather sufficient details to clarify special areas of concern regarding the management of particular programmes, including problems of communication between central and peripheral staff.

When formulating recommendations, the team should consider solutions suggested by the district health staff.

Supervision

The coverage and quality of supervision of PHC programmes by district personnel should be examined. Is there a good system of supervision? One of the signs of a good system is the existence of

Table 22. Dummy table to show frequency of supervision

Health facility	No. in district	No. of times visited during past year by district staff				
		>12	6–11	3–5	1–2	0
Government health centres						
NGO health facilities						
Government dispensaries						
Community health committees						
Community health workers						

Table 23. Table to show follow-up action after supervisory visit[a]

Health facility or body	Problems identified	Action taken	Level at which action was taken
Government health centres	Use of services poor because hours inconvenient for population	Established evening clinics for MCH services	Health centre
NGO health facilities	Using nonstandard schedule for immunization	Discussed reasons for standard schedule with staff	Referred to national NGO coordinating group for follow-up
Government dispensaries			
Community health committees	Not fully aware of health issues and activities undertaken in the community; hence, no support provided, and no active role	Discussed with chairman and referred problem to district development committee	District development committee with ministry of interior to organize sensitization sessions
Community health workers			

[a] This table is partly completed as an example of the kinds of answers that might be expected.

planned arrangements for supervision. Details of such arrangements may vary according to how widespread the district network of health facilities is and the number of available supervisors. The team should assess whether the prevailing system of supervision provides adequate contact and communication between district programme managers and the most peripheral service outlets (see Table 22).

Another sign of good supervision is the existence and use of job descriptions, checklists, and supervision reports. The team should ascertain the types of problem that have been identified following supervisory visits, the follow-up action taken and by which level. The reviewers could also assess the impact of supervisory visits from the central level, including whether they have generally facilitated resolution of problems in programme management (see Table 23). Discussions should be held on how to improve supervision.

Supplies

This part of the review is concerned with assessing the functioning of the supply system at the district level—whether it is actually working as it is supposed to do according to the central plan, and whether it is meeting the needs of the district.

In many countries, it is the responsibility of national managers to draw up standard drug lists, to arrange for the transportation of supplies to district depots or peripheral facilities, and, in general, to make sure that essential drugs and vaccines for all health activities are available throughout the country. The role the district plays in the distribution of supplies from the central to the peripheral level should be examined. Is there a district depot? Does it constitute a bottleneck? How often are supplies received from the central supply department? Is this according to schedule? Do the district staff have to travel to the central store or another place to obtain supplies? Have planned activities of the programmes been disrupted because of shortages of drugs, vaccines, or other essential supplies?

Resources for supplies are always limited. Therefore, district health authorities are responsible for ensuring that the supplies available are used efficiently, that the record system can predict problems, and that storage facilities and arrangements are adequate. The district depot should be visited in order to observe the adequacy of the storage and security arrangements to prevent wastage, and the stock control systems used to anticipate shortages of essential drugs, vaccines, etc. Through both observation and discussion, problems should be identified and suggestions for solutions solicited. A useful document that covers all aspects of logistics is "How to assess health services logistics with particular reference to peripheral health facilities" (unpublished WHO document SHS/85.9), which is available on request from Strengthening of Health Services, World Health Organization, 1211 Geneva 27, Switzerland.

Specific PHC elements

The team should determine which priority technical programmes need in-depth review at this level and select appropriate questions and survey methods. The review should be especially aimed at assessing whether there is a proper balance between programme staffing and other resources at the district level.[a]

---

[a] The following manuals and publications provide useful guidance in this respect: *Evaluate vaccination coverage*. An EPI training manual in the series "Training for the mid-level manager" (unpublished WHO document; available on request from Expanded Programme on Immunization, World Health Organization, 1211 Geneva 27, Switzerland); *Acute respiratory infections: a guide for planning, implementation and evaluation of control programmes within primary health care* (unpublished WHO document WHO/RSD/86.29; available on request from Control of Acute Respiratory Infections, World Health Organization, 1211 Geneva 27, Switzerland); Rotem, A. & Fay, J. *Self-assessment for managers of health care: How can I be a better manager?* Geneva, World Health Organization, 1987 (WHO Offset Publication No. 97).

A basic list of some key indicators is given below. For each indicator, state the year to which it applies and the source. (It may be desirable to ask about the past two or three years, in order to be able to reach conclusions about trends).

1. (Population with safe[a] water in the home or
   with reasonable access/Total population of
   district) $\times 100$ $= ——\%$

2. (Population with adequate[a] facilities for excreta
   disposal/Total population of district) $\times 100$ $= ——\%$

3. Immunizations performed in last five years (infants
   and pregnant women)
   Tabulate these numbers as shown below:

Immunization	19. .	19. .	19. .	19. .	19. .	Trend[a]
BCG						
DPT1						
DPT3						
Polio 1						
Polio 3						
Measles						
Tetanus toxoid 1						
Tetanus toxoid 2						
No. of births (target population)						

[a] Conclusion on trend:
    + + = Significant increase (number of immunizations at least doubled in the last 5 years)
    + = Moderate increase (number of immunizations increased by at least 25% in the last 5 years)
    0 = No increase (increase is less than 25%)
    ? = Unknown

4. (Population with access to local care and essential
   drugs/Total population of district) $\times 100$ $= ——\%$

The criteria involved are:
— Availability of treatment for common diseases
  and injuries.
— A regular supply of essential drugs. (Is there an
  uninterrupted supply of the drugs designated
  by the country as essential? To all parts of the
  district?)
— Is there a health facility within one hour's
  walk or travel for everyone in the district? (If

[a] In accordance with national definitions.

data on time taken are not available, but distance is, distance can be converted into time. For example, under many circumstances, it is possible to walk 5 km or to travel 25–50 km by motor transport in one hour, depending on road or track conditions. Conversion factors can be calculated according to the terrain.)

5. Expected number of births (n) in the district (crude birth rate × population) (state year)   = —

6. (Number of pregnant women seen by trained personnel/n) × 100   = —%
Disaggregation according to place of care (home or health centre) and type of personnel is recommended. The average number of prenatal visits should be calculated and compared with the national norm (if there is one). The type of training of the personnel should be described.

7. (Number of deliveries attended by trained personnel/n) × 100   = —%
Disaggregation according to place of delivery and type of personnel is desirable. The rate, together with the data on the place of delivery (home or health centre or referred) and type of training (nurse, midwife, CHW, TBA), should be compared with any national norms, to determine whether the situation is satisfactory.

8. (Number of infants seen by trained personnel/n) × 100   = —%
The average number of infant visits/contacts and the type of care provided (including level of training of personnel) should be compared with any national norms to determine whether the situation is satisfactory.

9. (Number of home-based records (growth chart/immunization card) distributed to infants/n) × 100   = —%

10. Percentage of newborn infants with birth weight of less than 2500 g   = —%

11. Percentage of children under 3 (or 5) years of age
who are below reference value of weight-for-age $\quad = \underline{\quad}\%$

12. (Number of reported cases of diarrhoea in children
under 5 years/Number of children under 5 years of
age) $\times 100$ $\hspace{4cm} = \underline{\quad}\%$

13. (Number of children under 5 years treated with oral
rehydration salts (ORS)/Number of reported cases
of diarrhoea in children under 5 years) $\times 100$ $\quad = \underline{\quad}\%$

14. (Number of children under 5 years treated with
home-made rehydration solutions/Number of reported cases of diarrhoea in children under 5
years) $\times 100$ $\hspace{4cm} = \underline{\quad}\%$

Transport

The extent of the awareness of district managers of national policies
on transport management and the extent to which these policies are
being put into practice should be assessed. The assessment should aim
to establish whether vehicles are being used and maintained efficiently
and what the budgetary arrangements are for the purchase and
maintenance of vehicles. How often programme activities have been
disrupted by lack of vehicles or lack of fuel should also be ascertained
and whether the district has authority to pay for emergency repairs or
the purchase of fuel. Other relevant questions include the following:
Are special vehicles assigned to special programmes? Are they also
used for other programmes? If transport problems have been disrup-
ting programme implementation, what solution has been suggested?

Monitoring and evaluation

All districts participate in the collection, analysis, and use of information for the national health information system. The review at the
national level will probably have brought to light some problems in
the implementation of the system. The causes of these problems should
be examined at this and more peripheral levels. For example, if district
reports to central level are not sent in on time, the reason should be
sought. Is there a delivery problem between the reporting health
facilities and the district centre, or is the problem inherent in the
reporting system? Is the system too cumbersome, or is it not well

understood by those who are operating it? How is the information system functioning in the different PHC programmes? What other information is collected (e.g., data from sentinel surveillance sites, special studies, and research projects)?

One common problem is that data may be collected, but not analysed or used. The team should seek evidence that the information collected is being used for planning and management and should find out whether there is feedback from central level to the district and from the district to the periphery. This should be clarified by discussions with the staff concerned and also by review of district records to see what is actually happening. Where appropriate data over a number of years, or from several subdivisions of the district, are available for comparison, a graphic method of presentation will have obvious advantages. Furthermore, a display of up-to-date graphs and charts is a sign that data are being analysed and probably used.

PART 4

Health centre level

Introduction

The following sections provide examples of issues that the team might consider while composing its own questions and questionnaires to be used in structured, yet flexible, interviews at the health centre[a] level. Preference should be given to simple and closed questions rather than open-ended and complex questions. As far as possible, answers should be precoded in order to facilitate subsequent analysis and, to some extent, to clarify questions. It may, however, be desirable to ask an overall open assessment question at the end of the interview to allow staff to give their opinions on what they consider to be important issues in their work.

---

[a] These guidelines may also be applied to a dispensary or clinic, if the issues and activities for which the particular unit is responsible are selected.

1. Demographic and other features of the catchment area

This part of the review is concerned with assessing the local health workers' knowledge of the geographical and other characteristics of the catchment area, the locations of the various units related to the health centre, and the social and health profile of the population, especially that of the various target and vulnerable groups (see Table 24).

The following questions could be asked: Do you know what the target populations are for your priority programmes? How many women are pregnant or eligible for family planning? How do you know this? Do you keep track of their visits? How do you do this? What are the other vulnerable groups in your area? What are their characteristics? Where are they located? (If possible, ask staff to show their location on a map.) How many individuals are there in each group? What do they suffer from (e.g., % of malnourished children)? What could or should be done?

Table 24. Dummy table to show population of health centre catchment area, by community and age group

	Population			%
	Rural	Urban	Total	
Community A				
Community B				
Community C				
etc.				
Total (catchment area)				100
High-risk target groups				
Children 0–11 months				
1–4 years				
5–14 years				
Women of child-bearing age 15–45 years				

The team may ask if the health centre has a map of the catchment area, indicating the location of communities and health facilities. It is important that the health centre has such a map. Should this not be the case, the team should ask the health centre superintendent to prepare one.

2. Organization of health services

The team should assess the organization of the health system in the area served by the health centre, with particular emphasis on the role of the health centre itself in the implementation of PHC. In the sections that follow, examples are given of issues that could be considered to determine whether information gathered at higher levels is confirmed by what is seen and heard at the operational level.

Health centre

The questions in this section are focused on the health centre and its activities, and particularly on its relation to the peripheral levels. Are its activities coordinated and comprehensive? Are all the essential services being provided? Does the health centre meet the health needs of the area? How much attention is given to identifying and meeting the needs of the least healthy members of the local population?

The team can also ask the health centre staff to provide the following information about the organization of the local health system:

- number of fixed subcentres in the area;

- number of mobile teams;

- number of community (village) health posts;

- number of TBAs;

- number of NGO health facilities;

- number of private health facilities.

How much interaction is there between the various units providing health care, including nongovernmental and private clinics? Do all communities have access to essential basic health care, as well as referral services when necessary?

Is the health centre adequately equipped, in terms of physical facilities, staffing, supplies, and transport, to provide supervision, support and supplies, and to accept referrals? If there is a national standard for staffing, does the centre meet the standard? If not, why not?

In countries where the ministry of health has attempted to stand-ardize health facility design and construction, the team can use the national standard to appraise the layout and construction of the centre. Is the layout conducive to efficient work and orderly movement of patients? How many maternity beds or other beds are there? Is there a laboratory? Are there radiographic facilities? How well are these facilities maintained?

Contributions of other sectors to health

The contribution or impact, either positive or negative, of programmes of other sectors on the health of the people can best be determined at the level at which the programme is implemented. It should be noted that even a health-promoting activity will not be effective if it is not properly implemented. For example, a programme to provide school lunches will not be effective if implemented in schools where the pupils are not from underserved or risk groups. In order to be able to formulate questions for this level concerning the operational plans of different sectors, critical issues should be identified with the help of the information obtained during the document review at the national level. The team may have listed programmes that are being imple-mented in a collaborative manner, aimed at the same area or target group. The team may also have a list of programmes that have implications for health.

The questions put to the health centre staff should focus on finding out how much they know about programmes that should be jointly implemented at this level and their involvement in such programmes. The team should also interview the officials of the sectors concerned, to see whether they are aware of the health implications of their programmes and to assess their attitudes towards collaboration at this level. The officials should also be asked whether health considerations have been given priority during the implementation of their pro-grammes. Recommendations for further improvement in collaboration should also be sought.

The team may start by determining how the programmes or activi-ties of different sectors (including NGOs) that have been identified as having an impact on health have been coordinated with the related health programmes or activities. The following are some examples: the agricultural sector may implement a programme to retain a portion of a food crop for local consumption (instead of exporting all of it) in an area where the health sector implements a programme on nutrition education or nutritional surveillance. A scheme to increase the number of latrines and safe water containers may be set up in communities where basic sanitation facilities are lacking, and be complemented by the implementation of a programme in the education sector, using the school as the centre, to inform and educate the people in the community on how to use them. The team should try to assess how such programmes are being implemented to improve the health of the people, whether they are being conducted in a well coordinated manner, and whether they spread conflicting messages.

Furthermore, the team should focus on programmes addressed to vulnerable groups, even though these programmes may not have defined health objectives and may not be implemented in an intersectoral manner. For example, is there a food-pricing policy designed to help the poor and, if so, are the poor really benefiting from it? Is a female education scheme being introduced in the areas with high fertility rates or infant mortality rates? Is the public works sector building roads to give easier access to health facilities?

Another aspect is the way in which intersectoral activities are being coordinated at this operational level. Is there a mechanism by which the officials of different sectors in the area make their operational plans together, trying to coordinate all the activities that will promote the health of the people, so that they are implemented in the right place at the right time? How is this mechanism working? Are the officials of different sectors satisfied with the existing collaboration? How would they suggest further improving intersectoral collaboration at this level?

Community involvement

The existence of active community involvement in health is an important measure of the stage reached by a health system in its reorientation towards the PHC strategy. Such involvement depends, in part, on the efforts and ability of the health centre staff to cultivate community interest and participation in health. The team should find out the strategies and methods that have been adopted by the health centre staff to promote community involvement. Do health centre staff attend community committee meetings, participate in community group meetings (e.g., women, youth), develop and maintain outreach work in communities, cooperate with the community in training CHWs and TBAs, or make home visits? Which activities of the health centre are scheduled in consultation with community leaders (e.g., MCH care sessions, immunization, nutrition activities, environmental health activities)? Which community groups are actually operating in the area, e.g., youth, women, religious, cultural? Has any committee or group in the community (e.g., NGO, women's group) assumed responsibility for the following activities: identifying cases of leprosy, tuberculosis, or malnutrition, or water sources needing protection; reporting epidemics; collecting and disseminating health information; mobilizing health action; collecting contributions for health programmes; discussing and planning health action; or constructing latrines? What progress has there been in strengthening community involvement in health over the past two years (much, a little, none)? Are there any examples of community involvement? If so, are these efforts successful?

3. Programme implementation

The following sections focus on assessing how the various PHC programmes are being implemented in the area covered by the health centre. While these sections are related to "Operational management of programmes" in Part 3 (district level), the emphasis and terminology at this level are deliberately directed towards programme operation. Some aspects of programme management (e.g., budget, planning), which were given prominent attention at the higher levels, should be touched on here only if the health centre has responsibility for them. Otherwise, the evaluation should be limited to the key elements in programme implementation, that is, general programme management, supplies, information support, and programme effectiveness.

General management of PHC programmes

The overall operation of programmes by the health centre, as the referral institution for the community and other peripheral services, should be reviewed by obtaining answers to the following questions. Which PHC programmes (see Table 25) are in operation? Are the national policy documents for these programmes available at the health centre? Is the health centre's operation of PHC programmes in line with national policy and guidelines? Is there a written plan of work for the health centre for the current year including a description of its activities and targets? If so, describe it. Do available job descriptions of the health centre staff include outreach activities and supervision of CHWs? Do staff know what is expected of them? Is this knowledge based on written information or hearsay? Is what they do in line with what the ministry of health says they should be doing? Do the health centre staff say they are generally satisfied with the work being done? If not, what are the main causes of dissatisfaction?

Supervision is an essential task of the health centre and a number of procedures in field supervision are expected to be followed by the health centre staff. The team should discover to what extent the following procedures exist at this centre: a schedule for supervisory visits by each staff member, a checklist for supervision, written reports on supervisory visits, mechanisms for discussion and follow-up of supervisory reports by health centre staff. Also the team should determine the number of supervisory visits made by health centre staff to subcentres and communities within the last month; the purpose and

Table 25. Dummy table to show programmes of health centre

Service/activity	Offered by health centre		Category of staff responsible	Frequency (per week, month, year)	Where offered		
	Yes	No			Health centre	Out-reach	Home
Prenatal care							
Delivery care							
Young child care							
Family planning							
Growth monitoring							
Food supplementation							
Health education							
School health							
Malaria control							
Water supply promotion							
Environmental health promotion							
Curative care							
etc.							

Note: The columns after the first one may not always be relevant. They are of value only if the findings can be compared with an agreed national model or standard (or several levels, e.g., health centre type 1, 2, or 3). The information collected can then be used to establish whether the health centre meets the standard or is below the standard, and in what respects.

frequency of visits to the health centre by CHWs and TBAs within the last month; and the number of supervisory visits made to the health centre from a higher level during the last three months, and by whom.

A description should be given of the training activities that have been provided for the health centre staff within the past six months. Training courses conducted by the health centre staff for community and other peripheral health workers in the past six months should also be listed (see Table 26).

Table 26. Dummy table to show in-service training courses and participants (19 . .)

Programme area	Course title	Types of personnel	Date	Number of participants

Many PHC programmes have manuals or modules describing how to review their operation, for example:

— *Evaluate vaccination coverage.* An EPI training manual in the series "Training for the mid-level manager" (unpublished WHO document; available on request from Expanded Programme on Immunization, World Health Organization, 1211 Geneva 27, Switzerland).

— *Acute respiratory infections: a guide for planning, implementation and evaluation of control programmes within primary health care* (unpublished WHO document WHO/RSD/86.29; available on request from Control of Acute Respiratory Infections, World Health Organization, 1211 Geneva 27, Switzerland).

— Rotem, A. & Fay, J. *Self-assessment for managers of health care: How can I be a better manager?* Geneva, World Health Organization, 1987 (WHO Offset Publication No. 97).

— Battersby, A. *How to assess health services logistics with particular reference to peripheral health facilities* (unpublished WHO document WHO/SHS/85.9; available on request from Strengthening of Health Services, World Health Organization, 1211 Geneva 27, Switzerland).

The team should determine which priority technical programmes need in-depth review at this level and select the appropriate questions and survey methods from these manuals. Key performance indicators should be selected to assess the health centre performance for each programme under review. Questions that may be asked include: What are the targets in this area for the immunization programme? To what extent have these been reached? What advice is given to the mother whose child has diarrhoea? (The team should check that the advice is correct.) Staff should also be asked to prepare oral rehydration salt solution or home-made solution, depending on national policy, and the team should check that it is done correctly.

Similar questions can be devised for other programmes.

A basic list of some key indicators is given below. For each indicator, state the year to which it applies and the source. (It may be desirable to ask about the past 2 or 3 years, in order to be able to reach conclusions on trends.)

1. (Population with safe[a] water in the home or with reasonable access/Total population of health centre catchment area) × 100   = _____%

2. (Population with adequate[a] facilities for excreta disposal at home or close/Total population of health centre catchment area) × 100   = _____%

3. Immunizations performed in last five years (infants and pregnant women)
   Tabulate these numbers as shown below.

Immunization	19. .	19. .	19. .	19. .	19. .	Trend[a]
BCG						
DPT1						
DPT3						
Polio 1						
Polio 3						
Measles						
Tetanus toxoid 1						
Tetanus toxoid 2						
No. of births (target population)						

[a] Conclusion on trend:
  + + = Significant increase (number of immunizations at least doubled in the last 5 years)
  + = Moderate increase (number of immunizations increased by at least 25% in the last 5 years)
  0 = No increase (increase is less than 25%)
  ? = Unknown

[a] In accordance with national definitions.

4. (Population with access to local care and essential drugs/Total population of health centre catchment area) $\times 100$ = ____%

   The criteria involved are:

   — Availability of treatment for common diseases and injuries.

   — A regular supply of essential drugs. (Does the health centre receive an uninterrupted supply of the drugs designated by the country as essential?)

   — Is the health centre within one hour's walk or travel for everyone in its catchment area? (If data on time taken are not available but distance is, distance can be converted into time. For example, under many circumstances, it is possible to walk 5 km or to travel 25–50 km by motor transport in one hour, depending on road or track conditions. Conversion factors can be calculated according to the terrain.)

5. Expected number of births (n) in the health centre's catchment area (crude birth rate $\times$ population) (state year) = ____

6. (Number of pregnant women seen by trained personnel/n) $\times 100$ = ____%

   The figure should be broken down according to place of care (home or health centre) and type of personnel. The average number of prenatal visits should be calculated, and compared with the national norm (if there is one). The type of training of the personnel should be described.

7. (Number of deliveries attended by trained personnel/n) $\times 100$ = ____%

   The figure should be broken down according to place of delivery and type of personnel. The rate, together with the data on the place of delivery (home or health centre or referred) and type of training (nurse, midwife, CHW, TBA) should be compared with any national norms, to determine whether the situation is satisfactory.

8. (Number of infants seen by trained person-
    nel/n) × 100   = ____%
    The average number of infant visits/contacts and
    the type of care provided (including level of training
    of personnel) should be compared with any national
    norms to determine whether the situation is satis-
    factory.

9. (Number of home-based records (growth chart/im-
    munization card) distributed to infants/n) × 100   = ____%

10. (Number of newborn infants with birth weight of
    less than 2500 g/Number of newborn infants
    weighed) × 100   = ____%
    The weighing scales should be checked with a stand-
    ard weight, such as a 2-kg bag of rice.

11. (Number of children under 3 (or 5) years of age, who
    are below reference value of weight-for-age/Number
    of children of same age weighed) × 100   = ____%

12. (Number of reported cases of diarrhoea in children
    under 5 years/Number of children under 5 years of
    age) × 100   = ____%

13. (Number of children under 5 years treated with oral
    rehydration salts (ORS)/Number of reported cases of
    diarrhoea in children under 5 years) × 100   = ____%

14. (Number of children under 5 years treated with
    home-made rehydration solutions/Number of re-
    ported cases of diarrhoea in children under 5
    years) × 100   = ____%

Supplies

This section is concerned with evaluating the efficiency of logistic
support for the operation of PHC programmes at this level. Examples
of unfavourable findings are: shortage of transport for distribution of
supplies; poor managerial control of supplies at the health centre;
pilfering and improper use of supplies at the health centre. These and
similar problems often reduce the effectiveness of many health centres. Using a few critical indicators, the team should determine the
situation with regard to management procedures for supplies at the
health centre, as well as current and past availability, storage, and use
of supplies.

Table 27. Dummy table to show situation as regards drug/vaccine supplies

Health centre . . . . . . [name]

Description of drug/vaccine	Amount received during 19 . .	Amount issued during 19 . .	Present stock on . . . . (date)	Amount required per month	Present stock will last . . . months
Chloroquine tablets					
Oral rehydration salts					
Penicillin for injection					
Tetracycline					
Iron/folic acid					
Aspirin					
Oral contraceptives					
Condoms					
etc.					

The following questions should be asked. Is there an integrated supply system for all programmes? Which programmes have their own arrangements for supplies? Is there a standard list of drug supplies and drug stocks for the health centre? What is the usual source of supplies (e.g., regional/district health administration centre, national supply department)? Are records of supplies up to date? Are they accurately kept? What problems have been experienced by the health centre staff in the past 12 months in maintaining an adequate stock of drug and vaccine supplies (e.g., insufficient supplies, budget, transport, fuel, inadequate system for distribution of supplies).

The completion of a table, such as Table 27, using about five items as indicators, serves not only to indicate the availability of selected essential items at the health centre but also to verify the records. A visit to the store should be made in order to confirm, or supplement, information obtained in the interview.

The team should consider the following questions: Are any stocks out of date or unusable? Has there been an improvement in the drug and vaccine supply situation in recent years? Has there been any loss of drugs from the health centre's store within the past 12 months? Have there been problems with the storage of vaccines and medicaments? Is there enough cold chain equipment to satisfy the needs of the EPI programme? (If not, describe the deficiency.) Is there a thermometer inside the vaccine refrigerator? On checking the thermometer, what does it show? Does it indicate satisfactory refrigeration? Check also the temperature records.

Information support and disease surveillance

This part of the review has two aims: to assess whether the health centre is collecting and using information on the programmes and activities under its responsibility (see Table 28), and to determine whether this facility is integrated into the national health information system. The team should investigate whether the community is involved, if not why not, and whether the health centre is a bottleneck in the movement of national health information. If so, what solution can be recommended?

One of the principal uses of health information is disease surveillance. The team should ask for information on the incidence and prevalence of diseases in order to assess the health centre's ability to use collected data. The 10 diseases most frequently diagnosed at the health centre in the past year should be listed in order of frequency. The team should not only examine available data and records, but also

---

Table 28. Dummy table to show reporting compliance, 19. .

	Sub-centres	CHWs	TBAs	Other	Total
A. Number of reports expected					
B. Number of reports received					
C. % of expected reports received ((B/A) × 100)					
D. Number of reports received within 1 month of due date					
E. % punctual reporting ((D/A) × 100)					

Note: Calculations for C and E to be made at the time of analysis.

observe whether such data have been analysed and displayed on charts and graphs, e.g., to show trends in incidence of important diseases, trends in immunization coverage, or progress in the use of ORS or home-made rehydration solutions.

From the data collected and analysed by the health centre, the team should see if there are examples of calculated rates, e.g.:

- percentage of fully immunized children (age . . .)
- percentage of women attending for prenatal care at least once during last or present pregnancy
- percentage of children with diarrhoea given ORS
- percentage of women in the 15–44-year age group using modern contraceptive methods

Note that some of these rates have already been requested (see pages 104–109). Questions need not be repeated when they serve more than one purpose (in this case as indicators for both programme management and the information system).

PART 5

Community health workers and traditional birth attendants

Introduction

This part of the review is concerned with all types of community health workers. As designations and job descriptions vary from country to country, the team should familiarize itself with the role, functions and designation of each type of worker. The roles played by each type of health worker are usually distinct, and it is preferable to prepare a separate questionnaire for each. The guidelines given here illustrate evaluation for the two most common categories, community health workers (CHWs), sometimes called village health workers (VHWs), and traditional birth attendants (TBAs).

The interviews should concentrate on what the CHW or TBA does, how well he or she performs, and what is required to sustain and improve performance, rather than compiling a vast amount of data that either are already known to national programme managers or will contribute little to the improvement of CHW and TBA performance. Where the PHC review is aimed mainly at a particular programme, the interview with the health workers should be oriented accordingly.

The information required will be obtained through a combination of observation and a structured, but flexible, dialogue with the worker. The team should design questionnaires for obtaining relevant data, preferably in a form that will facilitate subsequent analysis. At the CHW level, the emphasis should be on simple, unambiguous, closed questions rather than open-ended or opinion-type questions (except for the final general discussion section). As an illustration of the way questions could be formulated, a questionnaire with sample questions for TBAs is provided in Annex 2.

1. Community health worker

Personal characteristics of CHWs

The performance, motivation, and continuity in employment of CHWs are often causes of concern to national health managers. This part of the review aims to identify the characteristics of good stable health workers, facilitate decision-making on modifications to arrangements for CHW support, training and supervision, and influence the future development of the cadre. The following issues could be considered: Is turnover more rapid among married or among single CHWs? Do illiterate CHWs prove more loyal and dedicated than literate ones? Are male CHWs more acceptable to their communities than female ones? Are factors such as age, present or previous occupation, or social status within the community of significance? Besides the obvious facts, such as name, age, sex, and marital status, the following information should be obtained from the CHW. What is the distance of your health post from the health centre? Were you born in this area? How long have you lived here? How long have you been a CHW? What was your work before you became a CHW? Do you have other work now as well as being a CHW? Can you read this? (Show a simple text.) How many years schooling have you had?

Information about the community

A thorough knowledge of the area and of the people and their problems is a basic prerequisite for effective operation. Thus, the team should discover how well the CHW knows his or her area and its people. Are there beliefs and practices within the community that may have either a positive or negative impact on health? What local facilities are available for the emergency transportation of patients to the health centre or hospital?

The CHW should be asked for basic information about the community including the following: What is the total population in your area? What is the total number of households? How many pregnant women are there in your area? (The team should use this opportunity to fill in any gaps in the knowledge of the CHW on these questions and to explain the importance of such basic information to his or her work.) What are the most common diseases and health problems in your area?

Have you ever taken part in studies to find out the problems and needs of your community? (If so, specify.) What is the most dependable means of transport available to you or your community for emergency use?

Selection and training of CHWs

This assessment should supplement the information already obtained about the personal characteristics of the CHW, by determining whether the method of selection and the type of training given have contributed to job satisfaction and performance. Information to be obtained should include whether a CHW who is selected by the whole community (or by representatives of various segments of the community) is more acceptable to the community than one nominated by the village leader.

As regards training, it would be relatively easy to review the content of CHW training through an interview. However, it is more important to assess the effectiveness and appropriateness of the training, as well as the quality of performance of the CHW. For example, does the CHW have sufficient knowledge and competence to deal with the prevailing health problems of the community? What practical training has the CHW had? Has the CHW had any further training since initial training? When and from whom? It may not be easy to arrive at firm conclusions on these issues without direct observation of CHW performance under real conditions, but the reviewers should try to achieve a realistic assessment.

Support, supervision, and working conditions

The CHW's perception of the quality of support received forms an important dimension of the review. Support should include not only working facilities and remuneration, but also supervisory support from both the health centre and the community, and demonstrable interest by the community in carrying out PHC activities. The following issues should be clarified: Does the health centre staff maintain a cordial and close liaison with the CHW? Has it been prompt in taking action to help find solutions to problems encountered by the CHW? Is the community actively involved in carrying out health-related activities in the area?

Questions such as the following might be asked: Has anyone from the health facility visited you recently? Who? When was the last visit? What was the purpose of this visit (e.g., supply, supervision, training, other (specify), don't know)? How many months ago was your most recent visit to your supervisory/referral health facility? What was the purpose of your visit (e.g., supplies, patient referral, advice, submit report, meeting, training, other (specify))? How many months ago did the village committee meet to discuss health matters? What was discussed? (Specify.) Are there volunteers or other staff in your community who work towards village development? If so, specify name and designation, and state which of them assist you in your health-related activities. Do you sometimes meet the other community workers to talk about your work in the community? Do you meet schoolteachers? Do you visit schools? Do you meet religious leaders to discuss problems of mutual concern? Does the village committee supervise the activities of all community workers? Is there any other coordinating body? Do you know of any messages or advice given to the community by another person that conflicts with your own health advice to the community? (If so, specify.) Has the community, in the past six months, organized and carried out any health-improvement activities? (If so, describe.) In which areas would you like to have better support from the committee? How many days did you actually spend on your CHW duties during the past week?

The remuneration of the CHW is one of the most problematic areas in PHC implementation. The team should, therefore, exercise tact in questioning the CHW about this matter, and it is preferable not to discuss the situation in the presence of community leaders, in order to obtain a true picture. Questions that might be asked include: Do you receive any reward or remuneration for your work as a CHW? In what form (e.g., certificate, uniform, money, goods, exemption from other community duties)? From whom? Are you satisfied with the arrangement? If not, a recommendation for a solution can be formulated, but preferably after hearing the community leaders' views. The team should also observe the physical state of the workplace of the CHW.

Routine activities

This section is intended to guide the team's assessment of the routine activities of the CHW, including his or her involvement in the implementation of PHC programmes as well as record-keeping and reporting. Is the range of CHW activities relevant to the health needs of the community? Does the level of competence appear to be satisfactory? What does the CHW do about any problems encountered? How does the CHW communicate with the community and its leaders for further action? Who helps to solve the problems encountered?

An examination of CHW records, if available, will give an idea of the scope of routine activities and their relevance to local needs. The examination of records should also give the team an opportunity to appraise the ability of the CHW to understand and use the records and to deal with common or serious conditions encountered.

The CHW may be asked the following: What are your routine activities? Which of them do you do most often? How many practising TBAs are there in your area? In which specific areas do you collaborate with the TBAs? Describe the immunization schedule. Do you weigh children yourself regularly? (The interviewer should ask to see the weighing scale and check its accuracy using a standard weight, such as a 2-kg bag of rice.) What is done with the weight data that you record? Is there malnutrition in your area? In which age group do you see most malnutrition? Does malnutrition occur mainly at certain times of the year? If so, which times? What do you do for severely malnourished children (e.g., refer to health centre, refer to hospital, help with village feeding, counsel mother and family, arrange extra food supply, other (specify) or "don't know")? Do you see children with diarrhoea? At which time of year is the number of cases highest? What is the main cause of childhood diarrhoea in your area? What is the cause of death in children who die with severe diarrhoea? How do you recognize dehydration (e.g., dry mouth, severe thirst, sunken fontanelle, sunken eyes, loss of skin elasticity, little/no tears or urine, weak pulse, weakness/collapse, other (specify), or "don't know")? Demonstrate how you make up ORS solution or a sugar and salt solution for the treatment of diarrhoea. (The interviewer should compare the latter with the local official formula.) What advice do you give to the mother of a child suffering from diarrhoea (e.g., continue with breast-feeding, give extra fluids, give ORS solution or sugar and salt solution, give medicaments (if so, do the medicaments given accord with national policy?), continue to feed child normally, feed child more frequently, watch for signs of dehydration, seek help if child not improving with sugar and salt solution, explain how to prevent diarrhoea in future, other (specify), or "don't know")?

Questions on environmental sanitation, health education, and record-keeping could include the following: What is the main source of drinking-water in the village? Is the supply of water sufficient all the year round? What is the most common method of garbage disposal in this area? Do people in this village use latrines? If not, why not? (The team should physically check the answers.) How many months ago did the community have a community cleanliness campaign? Do you and/or the community do anything about malaria control (e.g., clear breeding sites/water pools, control adult mosquito population by spraying, control larval mosquitos by larviciding, use bednets and/or window screens, drug treatment, other (specify), or nothing)? What health education activities have you undertaken during the past six months (e.g., general health promotion, nutrition, breast-feeding, diarrhoea control, safe water, sanitation, family planning, immunization, other (specify), none)? Do you keep records? If so, are they periodically collated and analysed? Are they analysed with the help of your supervisor? Are they discussed with your supervisor? (The team should examine the records.)

Supplies and equipment

The credibility of the CHW and the programme often depend heavily on the regular availability of essential supplies and equipment. The team should discover whether the health post has a stock of these essential items. Are items under- or over-stocked? Are they safely and systematically kept?

Questions that might be asked include the following: Have supplies of any items run out during the last three months? What were the items and what were the reasons for the shortages? Where does the CHW obtain new supplies? Are there any other (nongovernmental) sources of drugs for the community? (If so, specify.) Does the CHW have a list of drugs and other supplies that are supposed to be in stock? The team should check this list against the actual supplies at the village health post. Can the CHW readily identify the different medicines in the drug cupboard or box? Does the CHW know what dosages of the drugs to give to different age groups and the side-effects of the drugs? While neatness and orderliness are signs of the proper management of equipment and drugs, the review team should be aware that supplies may be neatly kept because they are not being used at all.

General discussion

Throughout this phase of the survey, the team should allow enough scope for the CHW to express his or her views on the various subjects discussed. The team should also use the opportunity to talk about areas crucial to the effective performance of the CHW. Areas of dissatisfaction, as well as unmet needs and difficulties, should be thoroughly investigated. Above all, the final result of the visit should be a strengthening of the morale of the CHW.

2. Traditional birth attendant

In many parts of the developing world, TBAs, whether formally or informally trained, take charge of between 50% and 80% of all births. Thus, it is important that time and effort should be allocated to assessing the training of TBAs, their knowledge of the management of pregnancy and delivery, and the quality of the support and supervision they receive. In many developing countries, most expectant mothers and children who are at "special risk" will fall within the area of influence of the TBA. The team should proceed with its task using a combination of observation and interview. A sample questionnaire for TBAs is provided in Annex 2.

Personal characteristics of TBAs

This part of the review is intended to assist in the identification of attributes that tend to make a good, efficient TBA. The information will be useful to national health managers in planning the future development of TBAs. The "drop-out" rate of TBAs is not usually found to cause as much concern as that of other health workers, partly because the TBA cadre is well established. On the other hand, there is an increased need for competent TBAs to help reduce maternal mortality in the rural areas of developing countries. The characteristics of TBAs that should be considered by the team include age, sex, marital status, number of children, and duration of residence in the area of work. The literacy status and level of schooling of TBAs are assuming increased importance in many countries.

Information about the community

The broad aim of this part of the review is to determine how much background knowledge the TBA has of the area and people. Is the TBA knowledgeable about the sociocultural structure of her[a] community? Does she know the beliefs and practices relating to pregnancy, childbirth, and child-rearing in her area? Does she know other persons

---

[a] Note that, in this section, the TBA is referred to as a female. However, it should be borne in mind that in some countries men are important contributors to traditional birthing practices, and that in these countries they should be included in the review.

in her area who are involved in activities related to child-bearing? Which groups in the community are unwilling or unable to use her services? Who and what are her potential resources within the area?

Selection and training of TBAs

The review team may want to use the following issues as a basis for composing questions to be used in the interview. How was the TBA selected? What kind of training did she receive? Was the method used to select the TBA for training acceptable to the community as a whole? Does the training programme leave gaps in the TBA's ability to cope with what is expected of her? What arrangements are there for further training?

Support, supervision, and working conditions

The quality of supervision received has a major influence on job satisfaction for any worker. The team should interview the TBA to discover possible weak points in this field. Is the TBA dissatisfied with the reward given to her for her services? Does the TBA complain about the attitude of the staff at the referral health centre? Is the TBA getting less than full cooperation from the village's CHW? Has the community provided appropriate transport for referral of emergency cases?

Routine activities

At this stage, the team gets to the core of the task of evaluating the role of the TBA. The extent to which the TBA is involved in family planning, immunization, nutrition, etc., should be ascertained. The complications of the third stage of labour, particularly postpartum haemorrhage, account for the majority of maternal deaths in the developing world. Regrettably, there is usually little scope for effective action by the TBA once the complication has set in. Perhaps here, more than at any other time, the TBA's powers of anticipation and quick judgement will decide whether the mother lives or dies. The TBA should be asked whether she can remember how many mothers died in the past month because of bleeding after delivery or because of fever after delivery. How many cases did she refer? Does she keep a record of such cases? Information should be collected about the knowledge of the TBA concerning the identification and management of high-risk cases and the following issues should be kept in mind when the team is observing the TBA's work or having a discussion with her. Is her level of competence adequate to deal with the complications of childbirth? Does she understand the purposes of data collection and record-keeping?

Supplies and equipment

At this stage, the team should assess the logistic support for the work of the TBA. Does she have all the essential equipment required to support her operations? Does she have sufficient supplies, according to the national standards? Is the TBA able to use the equipment provided? The interviewers should also observe the TBA's equipment, in order to compare what is seen with what is reported. If the TBA says that she weighs babies after birth, does she have an appropriate scale for this purpose? If so, is it accurate? (The interviewer should check with a standard weight, such as a 2-kg bag of rice.) Does she have scissors or a razor blade for cutting the cord? Does she have soap and basin for hand-washing prior to conducting a delivery? A neat and tidy TBA is more likely to use clean techniques than a disorganized one.

General discussion

The team should allow enough scope for the TBA to express her views on the various subjects discussed, and should use the opportunity to inform and educate her about areas crucial to effective performance. Areas of dissatisfaction, as well as unmet needs and difficulties, should be thoroughly addressed. Above all, the visit should result in encouragement and strengthening of morale for the TBA.

Community leaders

Introduction

This part of the review is concerned with community leaders in the communities and villages selected for the PHC survey. Before commencing the field work for this phase of the survey, the team and the interviewers should select the community leaders who will be questioned, depending on the national or local situation. The choice will usually be among the community chief or head, the chairman of the village committee, a religious leader, the local member of parliament, the chairman of the local cooperative society, heads of local women's and youth organizations, etc. The agreement on the community leaders to be interviewed should be adhered to as closely as possible, and any departure from it should be indicated in the findings. The purpose of the interviews is not to get information about the community leaders themselves, but rather to determine what they perceive as priority health problems, what they do about these problems, and to what extent the community is supporting and contributing to primary health care and other health activities.

Most countries have considerable experience of interviews at the community level. The community should be given ample advance notice of the survey, and discussions should start with a meeting with one or several community leaders. Depending on the scope of the survey, it may be possible to obtain all the information required at this meeting. Alternatively, it may be necessary to interview community leaders at a subsequent session. The interview should consist of a combination of directed discussions, group interviews, and the observation of behaviour during the meetings, as well as a number of structured questions with a limited number of options for answers. Interviewers should always clearly understand the points that they want to establish through question, discussion, or observation. This should be emphasized during their training.

It is advisable to avoid questions on subjects that do not have a direct bearing on PHC services, especially if the subjects are considered to be of a delicate or controversial nature. On the other hand, where it is known that the ministry of health is formulating a new policy or programme in a certain field, detailed questioning can be used to explore the community's attitude to the proposal. If a programme is being implemented, it may be opportune to ask community leaders appropriate questions aimed at appraising community involvement.

The success of community-based and community-supported primary health care, in the final analysis, depends on strong and sustained community involvement. Two major goals of this part of the review should be to assess the strength of community motivation towards PHC and to look at the resources that the community could use to meet its commitments under the PHC strategy. This is also an opportunity to evaluate the community's organizational structures in relation to its involvement in health and health-related matters, and to investigate health and health-related services in the community, such as sanitation, water supply, proximity to a health care facility, transport to a referral facility during emergencies, etc. The team should coordinate this part with the evaluations described in Part 5 (Community health workers and traditional birth attendants) and Part 7 (Household level).

1. Community organization

The broad aim of this part of the review is to determine whether there is suitable and effective community organization. It is generally found that success in getting a community involved in the development and operation of PHC, and its component programmes, depends primarily on the community leaders and the extent to which their views are harmonized. This harmonization of views is especially important when a community consists of groups with different interests. A good system of community organization will go a long way towards bringing about the desired harmonization. The central level may know which communities have a committee or some other mechanism for collective decision-making in matters concerning health, other social and economic activities, and/or local government affairs. This information should be confirmed through such questions as: Is such a committee statutory and multipurpose? How are its members chosen? If there is no committee, how are community decisions made?

2. Perception of health problems and health services

This part of the review is concerned with determining the level of the community's awareness of its health problems, and what is being done towards their solution. The community cannot be expected to be motivated to implement a particular health activity, or even support such an activity, unless it is convinced that the activity concerned will meet a need. The interviewer should ask the following questions. What are the most serious prcblems? Who is most affected, and why? What do community leaders suggest to improve this situation? Which new health activity or programme would the community leaders like to see started in the area, in order to meet a particular problem? What have they done already? Do they collect data? What is their opinion about the services provided?

3. Community resources and self-reliance

The commitment of the community to the implementation of PHC should be appraised. Community commitment to PHC in practical terms means appropriate allocation of resources and self-reliance. To assess this, the following questions may be asked: Has the community: diagnosed its health problems? set its priorities? identified required resources? harmonized its objectives with those of the health services, in order to achieve self-reliance? Are there examples of the community organizing and carrying out health or health-related activities on a voluntary and self-help basis? Which community groups ought to do more for the health of the people?

4. Community health workers

A detailed evaluation of community health workers, including traditional birth attendants was considered in Part 5. Here, the team should assess, in particular, community satisfaction with the work of the CHWs/TBAs and community support for these workers. Support entails not only exercising adequate supervision over their services, but also providing appropriate social recognition and financial and other rewards. If it is found that the relationship between a CHW/TBA and the community committee is strained, the team should search for possible causes. Is it because the community is not providing remuneration in cash or kind, or is it because the committee is not exercising its supervisory authority? If the problem seems to be mainly on the side of the committee, the team might wish to recommend, to the national committee, ways of improving or strengthening the local committee.

5. Contribution of other sectors to health

An assessment should be made of the way different sectors are working with the people, and the extent to which they are producing complementary results; also how the community is organized to deal with overall community development. The interviewers should find out from the community leaders whether different sectors have their own community workers, and whether they are working solely within their sector or whether they are consulting with each other and coordinating their work. They should also find out whether any mechanism exists in the community to deal with overall community development activities, by coordinating the different workers or dealing with officials of different sectors where there are no community workers. Are workers from the different sectors carrying out similar activities?

The community leader might be asked whether he or she has been informed by the relevant sectors that their programmes are meant to complement each other. Does the community leader feel that programmes are implemented in a well coordinated way? Are they producing the results they are meant to achieve? Questions might be designed for the specific programmes implemented in the community. For example, if food prices are subsidized, are the poor able to buy food at these prices? If families receive poultry from the agricultural workers, do they raise them for their own consumption, as intended, or do they sell them and buy something less nutritious? Are there any credit schemes? If so, who benefits from them? Are there women's programmes, functional literacy programmes? Are these programmes run by the government, an NGO, or are they private? Which NGOs are working in the area? What do they do?

Annex 3 gives an example of a questionnaire for community leaders.

PART 7

Household level

Introduction

In this part of the review, information is collected from members of the community, usually in the context of an interview in the home together with observations made by the interviewer. In PHC evaluations and other studies, household surveys are often the only reliable way to get crucial data for the population as a whole, such as indicators of health status, coverage of health services and essential PHC elements (e.g., immunization, sanitation, water supply), use of health facilities, and some of the global health-for-all indicators.

The interviewer should pose questions to a well-informed adult in the household (referred to as "respondent" in the rest of this section); this will often be the woman of the household. Data should also be obtained from visual observation. At this level, the questionnaires should be as short, structured and unambiguous as possible, so that data can be obtained uniformly and efficiently, even when interviews are conducted in several languages.

It is still very difficult to get information where it matters most—at the household level. However, it cannot be emphasized enough, especially at this level, that information should not be collected just for its own sake. The issues to focus on should be determined in the light of national concerns and the selection of critical indicators for these issues is crucial. In short, the most important criteria for selecting indicators are: Are they relevant for policy decisions and for monitoring progress, can they be acted upon, and is it feasible (technically, financially and managerially) to gather the information required? The following are the main types of issue to be considered at this level:

- *Social and economic determinants*, including intersectoral action and community involvement. These factors reflect the state of development in other key sectors that directly or indirectly influence health.

- *Provision of health care.* Aspects to be considered are accessibility, acceptability, affordability, quality, and utilization of services, as perceived at the household level. It should be noted that the same information may also need to be looked at from the point of view of the health institutions.

- *Health programme indicators.* These may be collected for programmes that are priority issues for the country review. Some of the indicators may be available from separate studies, while for others the household survey is the only appropriate means of obtaining the data. The need for some types of household data collection may also decrease as the quality and coverage of the routine health information system improve.

1. Methodological considerations

Sampling procedures

Sampling procedures for PHC reviews are usually based on the household as the basic sampling unit. In general, some element of clustering will also be involved. Procedures for sampling are described in detail in Annex 1, where reference is made to the possibility of needing grossly different sample sizes for different items or indicators, in order to achieve the desired level of precision of the estimates. For example, a question on diarrhoea morbidity may require a sample size four times as big as a question on immunization. If, in such a situation, it is not practical to ask all the questions in all households in the large sample, a systematic subsample (in this case, every fourth household) can be taken for the question for which a smaller sample size suffices. But this should be done only with much caution as it considerably increases the complexity of the survey.

Furthermore, it is of paramount importance that the review team is aware of the fact that, because of the relatively small number of households in each cluster, no conclusions can be made about the individual clusters. Conclusions can be drawn only from regional or countrywide results, depending on the answers given. Clustering and sample size also limit the possibility of drawing conclusions about interrelationships between different items on the questionnaire (such as number of deaths versus quality of housing).

Finally, it should be emphasized that conditions that occur rarely or measures that show large variations in the population also require very large samples for precise estimation. Examples are: infant mortality, disease-specific mortality or the use of oral rehydration. In most cases, a manageable sample size for a quick review will be too small to permit reliable and precise values to be obtained for these indicators. In such cases, questions related to this type of indicator should not be included in the questionnaires.

Household interviews

For the whole stage of data collection in the field, most of the available time, resources and manpower will be invested in the assessment at the household level. It is at this level that the impact of all aspects of PHC on health status is seen and should be measured. As mentioned above, large numbers of households must be included to arrive at estimates with an acceptable precision. The reliability of an estimate depends not only on the sample size but also on the quality and the reliability of each individual answer, and thus very much on the way the questions are asked. Proper training of the interviewers is therefore of paramount importance, especially for the interviews at this level. (More details about interviewer training can be found in Part 1.) A well designed questionnaire, which is both selective and specific, is important to save time and obtain reliable data. It is also important that interviewers know how to ask questions appropriately and that the respondent is motivated to participate in the interview.

The interviewer has to be able to put the questions in such a way that they will be understood by the people, using their languages and local expressions, or to modify the questions as necessary without distorting their meaning. She or he also has to be able to create a good atmosphere. Motivation for participation may be increased by giving the respondent commonly used household remedies, packets of oral rehydration salts (ORS), educational material, etc.

Making the interview session an educational one is also an interesting and useful way of motivating the respondent. An interview at this level should have an educational objective so that relevant health information and knowledge are delivered to the respondent, as appropriate and necessary, e.g., about the proper use of ORS, or how to deal with certain diseases. Although this will prolong the interview, it is an aspect that should be considered; time should be set aside and the interviewers informed about this educational objective in planning for work at this level. Note, however, that care should be taken not to bias the respondent. It may be desirable to postpone the educational activities until after the formal interview.

Questionnaires

As has been said earlier, selectivity must be the keynote. Priority issues and a few selected indicators relevant to the country should be identified. Another reason to keep the questionnaire short is that respondents may be reluctant to participate or give answers, or may withdraw from the interview if it takes too much of their time.

More will be gained by selecting a small number of relevant indicators for which information can be obtained within a reasonable time than by aiming at comprehensiveness. The questions should be as clear and unambiguous as possible, and simple enough for the questionnaire to be very structured, with pre-coded answers, so that analysis is feasible for the large number of sampling units that are needed at this level.

Forms A and B in Annex 4 are examples of household and immunization coverage questionnaires. Form A is an example of a questionnaire for use in every household in the cluster. The 10 columns make it possible to cover 10 households with one single form. It should be noted that, with this design, only pre-coded answers can be checked and there is little room for writing down replies that differ from what is expected. The advantages of this format are that the interviewers will have to carry fewer forms with them on their field trips and that analysis is relatively easy. However, this design is not necessarily the most appropriate in all circumstances. In most situations, a shorter list of questions would be advisable; a longer list of questions is certainly not recommended. The questions in this example cover a variety of issues: general characteristics, utilization and awareness of health and other related services, immunization, diarrhoea, malaria, housing, and mother and child care (the last issue to be reviewed only when a child under 5 years of age is present). Questions on certain issues (such as malaria, housing, and diarrhoea) should be asked only if a relevant programme exists and/or action can be taken with regard to the situation encountered, if necessary.

Form B, widely used for measuring immunization coverage, is concerned only with children in the cluster aged 12–23 months.

It is most important that questions should be asked only if they are of direct relevance to the current situation and if the information cannot be obtained from other sources. The questions should be grouped around particular issues, topics or programmes and listed in a logical sequence. The questionnaire should begin with some simple questions to make the respondent feel comfortable, with the more complicated or delicate questions coming later.

Some of the issues that might be considered at the household level are looked at more closely below. Note that the questionnaires in Annex 4 do not necessarily follow the same sequence of issues. Neither the issues considered here nor the questionnaires are meant to be comprehensive or mandatory, but are meant to stimulate the process of selecting the most critical indicators for the relevant priority issues, and to provide a sample of questions that have been used in a number of surveys and found to be satisfactory.

cial and economic determinants

Social and economic factors are generally recognized as important determinants of health. At the household level, they can reflect the state of development in other key sectors influencing health. They can help to identify the vulnerable or underserved population in areas of economic, educational, or social development, using indicators such as employment, income level, literacy, agricultural productivity or wages. If the sample has been designed properly, these indicators can be analysed according to subpopulations of different health status or with different levels of PHC development. (Cross-analysis may only be possible if the sample has been specially designed for the purpose.)

Employment and income levels

When surveying heterogeneous regions, it may be relevant to look at employment conditions and sources of income. This may help to explain differences in health status in different subgroups, because, for example, risk factors for a food-producing population will be very different from those for communities that derive their income from industrial labour. Indicators that reflect employment status might include the level of unemployment or underemployment and the percentage of women in the labour force. However, these indicators are less useful in countries where most people are self-employed or in the informal sector, and it may be sufficient simply to ask about their sources of income. Ownership of land, cattle, bicycles, radios, motor vehicles, television, and other possessions reflecting wealth, and means of earning income are proxy indicators for income distribution. All these may shed light on the possible risk factors influencing the health of the people.

Adult literacy

Education is likely to have a strong influence on progress towards health for all. One possible indicator of the contribution of education to health is the literacy rate, particularly among women, since it is they who most often take care of the basic health needs of the family. It is also an indicator of social equity. Literacy can be looked at in terms of number of years of schooling or functional capacity to read.

142

Housing

Housing is also likely to have a considerable effect on health. The most commonly available indicator of the adequacy of housing is the number of persons per room. Housing indicators should take into account the nature of the accommodation in terms of its size, its insulation against extremes of weather, the availability of water and sanitary facilities, the presence of animals, ventilation, cleanliness of the surroundings, etc. The exact criteria for each of these components for "acceptable" or "adequate" housing will have to be determined according to the country or local situation. The absolute value of the indicator is less important than changes in the indicators over time. It will be particularly relevant to look at the housing situation in countries where there is a housing programme and thus where it is possible to act upon the findings.

Note: Data on housing may be obtained by using a checklist of observations rather than by posing questions.

Water

Water is an important determinant for health. The existence of a water-point is no guarantee, in itself, that water will always be available and safe. Also, a water-point requires drainage, otherwise the provision of water can have adverse health effects. In the absence of a water-point in the household, another indicator is the availability of a standpipe or protected well within a given walking time from the home, for example, 15 minutes. Is this water available all year round? If more in-depth information is desired, the water-storage facilities in the households might be looked at, as well as how water is treated before it is used for drinking, especially where children and infants are concerned.

Food and food security

Food availability and habits, and food policies, prices, and programmes are closely related to the health of the population. What type of food is being consumed most? Are other nutritious foods available and afford-able? Are there subsidies on certain foods? What programmes exist to control food prices? Are there programmes that promote the cultivation of nutritious plants, the rearing of poultry, etc.? Is there a programme on supplementary feeding for children? Is there preferential treatment for either boys or girls?

It is important to find out which subpopulations are covered by, and benefiting from, these programmes. Are they the ones really in need, the most vulnerable groups? For example, a certain food-pricing policy may not result in better availability of food for the poor, because they still may not be able to obtain food in adequate amounts, or low-priced food may not be accessible to them. As another example, a poultry-rearing programme may not contribute to better nutrition if the products are all sold on the market and not consumed by the producers.

Other factors

Depending on the country situation and the objectives of the survey, it may be desirable to find out the contributions to health of other sectors and other factors than the ones already mentioned. It may also be worth while to take a closer look at the dissemination by different sectors of information with health implications for educational or promotional purposes.

For example, does the agricultural sector give information on the proper use and handling of pesticides to avoid their toxic effects? It is also useful to see whether other sectors are providing competing, conflicting or complementary messages or advice regarding health promotion. This could be done by inquiring at the household level about the types of messages given by workers from other sectors, e.g., agricultural workers, social workers and teachers, especially with regard to messages that are directly related to health.

Finally, cooperative schemes might be looked at, where they exist, and especially approaches adopted to encourage people to participate in health development activities. For example: Do people agree with the financial resource mobilization in their community? Do they have problems in providing their contribution? Do they benefit from the existing community financing scheme? Have they ever joined in a collective activity to improve community health? Are they satisfied with their community health workers? Are community meetings held regularly?

These issues are not easy to assess and reliable indicators have not yet been developed. It is also difficult from a brief interview to obtain answers that reflect the actual situation. Nevertheless, community involvement is a crucial part of primary health care and might even be assessed by using subjective judgements of the community itself.

3. Provision of health care

To gather data on the accessibility, utilization, and quality of health care is complicated. It would be convenient to have a composite indicator of the provision of health care, so that it could be said, for example, that 75% of the population is provided with good quality care. This would provide an indicator of coverage in the most general sense of the word. But no satisfactory indicator of this kind exists at the moment and it is necessary to break down this general concept of coverage or health-care provision and try to construct good indicators for particular aspects. One way of doing this is to separate the different levels of the health system (e.g., first level of health care as distinct from referral levels); another way is to look at different programmes, e.g., mother and child care, immunization, sanitation. Another type of breakdown distinguishes different measures of provision in terms of such concepts as accessibility and utilization.

Accessibility

For the measurement of accessibility, it may be useful to look at different aspects.

Physical accessibility

Physical accessibility of services is a first priority. It is useful to select a few priority services relevant to primary health care—for example, water supply, maternal and child care, and first-level curative care—and establish physical accessibility criteria for each of these. Each country will have to decide how to define "accessible": for example one hour's walking time, or half an hour's travel by ox cart. This may vary for different parts of the country and will be different for different types of services. Care during childbirth, for example, may have to be much nearer home.

Note that very often physical accessibility can be better assessed at the community level than at the household level, unless communities are quite scattered and sparsely populated.

Economic and cultural accessibility

Economic accessibility is related to the ability of the individual or the community to cover the cost of care; if a service is available but neither the individual nor the community can afford it, then it is not accessible.

Cultural accessibility is the acceptability of the services to those for whom they are provided: for example, in some societies, female health workers are preferred to male health workers to care for women. Acceptability also implies that services are seen to be relevant to priority needs, and offer care of adequate quality.

Utilization of services

Utilization of specific services, or actual coverage, is expressed as the proportion of people in need of a service who actually receive it in a given period, usually a year; for example, the proportion of children at risk who are immunized, the proportion of pregnant women who receive prenatal care or have their deliveries supervised by a trained attendant, or the proportion of people needing medical treatment who actually go to the health facilities. This is particularly relevant when assessing first-level health facilities. It is also important to find out about referral to higher levels of care. Do people use them on their own initiative or on the advice of the health workers at the first level of care? Are there any problems with being referred by and to the different levels of care?

It may be found that people are not making proper use of the facilities, especially the first-level ones. When people are not using the services, it is essential to find out the reasons. In some cases, facilities exist but people do not use them because of the lack of drugs or because the facilities are open at hours when people are occupied in the field or factories. Also, people may be attracted by the prestige of a more distant hospital, and may use it for care that could have been provided by local primary health care facilities. In many countries, it will also be relevant to look at the utilization of alternative services, traditional healers, etc.

Quality of health care

Ideally, indicators of coverage should be supplemented by indicators of quality of care, although utilization is itself a reflection of the quality of care. Quality control, however, is complex and requires a profile of a number of indicators. It is essentially required for managerial and supervisory functions, particularly at the district level. Although most of the information on quality of care will probably be collected at community level, a number of indicators might be developed to be incorporated in the household questionnaire in the form of a checklist or simple scoring system, e.g., the type of information given to the mother about certain issues, such as immunizations, diarrhoea control. Who gave this information? How many prenatal examinations did the mother receive? Was the child weighed at birth?

4. Health programme indicators

As noted above, coverage is really meaningful only if it relates to specific types of services. The following are some examples of indicators related to essential components of primary health care.

Health education

It is important to try to collect data from the household on "health literacy", namely an elementary understanding of nutritional and health needs and of how to prevent or control common health problems. The team may take into consideration the national or local programmes that include health education and then gather more in-depth information about health literacy in these particular areas by asking such questions as: What is the understanding of the problem? Has people's behaviour changed? (It must be emphasized that a high degree of understanding of problems and ways of solving them is not in itself an indicator of attitudinal and behavioural change.) Who or what was the main source of information dissemination (for example, mass media, health workers, the people themselves)?

Immunization

The indicator used is the percentage of children at risk immunized against the major infectious diseases of childhood that can be prevented by immunization. Many countries have experience with the widely used, standardized and well tested method of collecting this information (see form B in Annex 4). The percentage of children fully immunized in the target age group is a proxy indicator of the utilization and coverage of health services in general; it indicates a minimum of three contacts between the health service and the child.

Nutrition

A useful indicator is nutritional status. Anthropometric measurements to assess the growth and development of young children are the most widely used indicators of the nutritional status of a community, and the information may be readily available from existing nutritional surveillance systems without having to be sought in a household survey.

Birth weight can be an important indicator of community nutrition (the indicator could be expressed as the number of children per 1000 live births whose birth weight is lower than 2500 grams). However, low birth weight may also be related to certain diseases (such as malaria) or to specific nutritional deficiencies (such as endemic goitre). Where supervision of births by trained personnel is low, it may be difficult to collect data on birth weight.

The mid-upper-arm circumference has been widely used in recent years to assess nutritional status. This is particularly useful in relation to height. It does have certain disadvantages in terms of accuracy, but is quite adequate for rapid community diagnosis, if not for monitoring individual child growth.

Maternal and child health, control of diarrhoeal diseases, and other programmes

As has been said before, when a programme is a priority issue, critical indicators have to be selected. For mother and child care there may be indicators that reflect the access to information on family planning and the percentage of mothers using the various contraceptive methods, or percentage of pregnant women receiving prenatal care, etc. For diarrhoeal (or any other) diseases, the indicators may reflect the load of the diseases concerned in children (including those who do not come for care) and the degree of prevention and control in the households.

Annexes

Annex 1
Sampling for primary health care reviews

1. Introduction

Decisions about sampling of households or individuals should take into account possible constraints, including the time and budget available for the complete survey, from the planning stage to the publication of results. Within these constraints, it is important to identify and define the basic sampling unit, which, for PHC surveys, will usually be the household. The sample size has to be considered. This is not so much a question of deciding on the optimum size, as of considering the quality of the information that will be obtained from the largest sample size that is possible with the physical and financial constraints. The structure of the sample will also be important. Usually some element of clustering will be involved, and the smaller the number of clusters for a given total sample size the less informative the data will be. Before any data are collected, it is important to ensure that they can be analysed in accordance with the purpose of the survey, using the chosen sampling scheme. Some thought should also be given to methods of data presentation including tables and graphs.

While it is important to take care regarding the size and structure of a sample, it is equally important to keep in mind the goals of a PHC review and not to let statistical considerations override them. The primary consideration at all times should be whether the data to be collected using a particular sampling scheme will be useful. This, in turn, has to be measured against the goals, resources, and other options available for the review. It will seldom be the case that one method is completely "correct" while another is completely "wrong". It is more likely to be a choice between the more and the less efficient, and occasionally between doing something only roughly or doing nothing at all. Certainly, the statistician can give guidelines and suggest basic criteria for assessing a sampling scheme, as in the following sections, but, in the end, the responsibility lies with the review managers to try to understand how different sample types and sizes will affect the quantity and quality of the information obtained. The aim is to obtain the maximum return for the resources invested.

2. Some basic concepts

The basic sampling unit

The household will usually be the basic sampling unit in a general PHC survey. Other basic sampling units are possible for other types of survey (see Table A1).

Table A1. Possible sampling units for various types of survey

Type of survey	Basic sampling unit
EPI	Index child aged 12–23 months
MCH	Recently pregnant woman
Nutrition	Index child aged 1–3 years (or less than 5 years)
Diarrhoeal disease	Index child aged less than 5 years (or less than 2 years)
Environmental health	Household and/or community
Use of health services	Household

The choice of basic sampling unit defines the target population of the survey. For example, when the index mother is chosen as the sampling unit, the variables studied in the survey will be properties of such mothers, or of the children of such mothers, or of the households containing such mothers. They will not, for instance, measure the properties of households in general.

For most of the sampling units there will be no convenient sampling frame. In other words, there will be no simple list that will enable a specific sample of units to be chosen without going into the field to do so. It will usually be possible to choose communities in the form of villages, census blocks, city blocks, islands, etc. Sometimes, lists of households will exist within these communities. However, it would be rare to find health records that are so complete and up to date that they contain the total current population of index mothers or children. Even if they do exist, there would be obvious dangers in using such records to choose a sample that will be used to assess the coverage and use of health care services.

On the other hand, if an acceptable method can be established for choosing households one by one, this will provide an indirect procedure for obtaining a sample of any of the within-household sampling units. Even if the main or sole purpose of a survey is to study one of the various possible sampling units listed in Table A1, there are still good reasons why the survey should be based on a sample of households. Thus, consideration is restricted in the following sections to methods for the selection of households as basic sampling units.

The problems of speed and economy usually rule out the selection of simple random samples of households, and some form of cluster sampling will be adopted, using natural groupings of households such as villages. It is possible and, for reasons of cost or shortage of time, often necessary, to introduce other stages of sampling. For example, districts may be chosen first, then villages within districts, and households within villages. These multistage sampling schemes are discussed on pp. 175–177. The simplest case, where villages are chosen directly, is considered in detail on pp. 157–165.

Different types of measure

In a PHC review survey, data will be collected on several different types of measure. Most frequently these measures will be rates. In sampling terminology there is a clear distinction between rates that are proportions and rates that are ratios.

A proportion is a rate in which the denominator is the total number of basic sampling units in the sample, or the sum of the number of basic sampling units in several clusters, as in a geographical region.

A ratio is a rate in which the denominator takes any other value: for instance, it may be the total number of some other unit, or the number of basic sampling units in some class that cuts across clusters.

The difference between a proportion and a ratio is important when sample sizes are being assessed and when data are being analysed. The distinction is most easily made by means of an example. Suppose the target population is composed of households (which means that the household will also be the basic sampling unit) and that it has been possible to obtain a simple random sample of households from the population as a whole. Then the proportion of that population that has a latrine will be estimated by:

$$\frac{\text{Number of households in the sample with a latrine}}{\text{Number of households in the sample}}$$

However, suppose that another purpose of the survey is to estimate the diarrhoea morbidity rate in children less than 5 years old. This can be estimated from the same sample as before by:

$$\frac{\text{Number of children less than 5 years in sample with diarrhoea}}{\text{Number of children less than 5 years in sample}}$$

The important difference from the previous situation is that the divisor is no longer the sample size; it is the number of children aged less than 5 years discovered in the sample when the survey is carried out, and its value is not known until the survey is completed. This introduces extra uncertainty in the estimation of the population value from a sample, and, for this reason, a ratio of this kind will give a less precise estimate than a simple proportion would for the same sample size.

Other types of measure may also be used in a survey. In a categorical measure, the response may fall into one of several different classes or categories (e.g., where did you go for treatment of your last episode of illness?). The categories may be naturally ordered (e.g., mid-upper-arm circumference in red, yellow, or green zone of arm type). Opinions may be recorded on an ordered categorical scale (e.g., agree strongly, agree, neutral, disagree, disagree strongly), but these are unlikely to be suitable for PHC reviews, because of difficulties in interpreting them consistently.

Numerical values may be recorded as discrete values (usually whole numbers, e.g., numbers of children or age in years) or as measures on a continuous scale (e.g., weight or height). Continuous measures are less likely to arise in PHC reviews, because of the time and equipment needed for precise measurement.

Quality of information: bias and uncertainty

The methods of data collection and analysis described below will provide unbiased estimates of population values. When an estimate is unbiased, it is then possible to assess the degree of uncertainty in the estimated value by means of the standard error (SE). Roughly speaking, there is a 95% certainty that the true value of a population parameter will lie inside the interval:

(estimate $- 2\,$SE) to (estimate $+ 2\,$SE).

This interval is known as the 95% confidence interval (some examples are given on pp. 165–175).

The magnitude of the standard error of any estimate depends on three things: the sample size (the smaller the sample, the larger the standard error), the structure of the sample (the more clustered the data, the larger the standard error), and the way that the measure being studied is distributed within the target population. No estimate should be quoted without giving the standard error. Even if a survey has been designed and a sample size chosen to give a specific precision (e.g., $\pm 10\%$ in estimating a proportion), the decisions about design and sample size will be based on predictions that are of uncertain reliability. The only safe indicator of the precision of an estimate is its standard error calculated directly from the survey data.

The practical application of each of the above concepts is discussed in detail below.

3. Selecting a sample of clusters of households

The selection of a sample of clusters of households can be done in several stages. The basic principles for deciding on sample size and structure and the methods for calculating estimates and standard errors will be demonstrated first for the simplest situation in which a selection of villages is made directly within a region and estimates are obtained for this region. The extension to several stages of sampling is straightforward and is described with examples in sections 6 and 7, pp. 175–177. The number of villages and households to be chosen is discussed on pp. 160–165. Here, only the method of selection is considered.

Choice of clusters

It will be necessary to have a list of all the villages in the region where the survey is to take place. It is frequently advantageous to arrange the order of villages on this list purposively. Suppose a survey of primary health care measures is to be carried out. There may be some prior information—a previous survey perhaps or records at health facilities—that might indicate villages with high scores and those with low scores. In this case, the list should be arranged from low to high scores (or high to low) before the selection is made. See pp. 170–174 for further details.

To make the selection, it is necessary to have a measure of the population size in each village. The ideal measure would be the number of households in each village but, assuming that the mean size of household will not vary greatly from one village to another, any general measure of population size will do. The cumulative population of the villages is then calculated, as shown in the third column of Table A2.

For the purposes of demonstration, suppose it is required to choose three villages from this list of ten. Divide 6700 (the total population of the villages) by 3 (the number of villages in the sample): $6700/3 = 2233$.

Table A2. Selecting villages for a cluster sample

Village	Population size	Cumulative population size
1	1000	1000
2	400	1400
3	200	1600
4	300	1900
5	1200	3100
6	1000	4100
7	1600	5700
8	200	5900
9	350	6250
10	450	6700

This number is the sampling interval. Choose a random number between 1 and 2233. Suppose the random number chosen is 1814. This should be compared with the cumulative list to identify the first village in the sample. Since 1814 is between 1601 and 1900, village 4 will be chosen. Now add the sampling interval to the initial random number to obtain the next sampling value: $1814 + 2233 = 4047$. Since this number lies between 3101 and 4100, village 6 is chosen. Now, to identify the third and last village for the sample, again add the sampling interval to the current sample number: $4047 + 2233 = 6280$, and village 10 will be chosen.

If the original list of villages is in completely random order, this systematic sampling procedure is equivalent to sampling with probability proportional to size (pps), and the samples obtained should be analysed as though they were selected by a random pps scheme. On the other hand, if the villages have been ordered according to some criterion that is expected to be related to their scores on various PHC measures, this will have the effect of stratifying the systematic sample and should lead to a reduction in standard errors (see pp. 170–175).

Sampling units other than households

A list of possible sampling units for various kinds of survey was given in Table A1. Usually, as part of a PHC review, information of several kinds will be required, each kind apparently needing a different sampling unit. It would be extremely inefficient to carry out a separate survey for each purpose, each time choosing a new sample consisting of the appropriate sampling units. The only sensible option is to use the household as the basic sampling unit and, for variables defined on different sampling units that appear in only some of the households, to estimate population values using the methods described for ratios on pp. 168–170 and 172–174.

For example, if the principal aim of a survey is to collect information on mother and child health, then the sampling unit of interest would be the recently pregnant woman (where "recently" would need to be defined). It would be possible to decide on the number of such women to be sampled in each village and to devise a method of sampling exactly that number. However, the calculation of unbiased estimates from this sample would then involve complicated formulae.

Thus, even if the purpose of a survey is to collect information on only one type of individual within a household, e.g., an index child or a recently pregnant woman, then a fixed number of households should still be selected in every village, even though the number of index children (or women) actually sampled will differ from one village to another. The number of households to be sampled should be chosen to give, on average, the number of index individuals required for the collection of data in each village. For example, if it is believed that roughly 40% of all households will contain an index child, and if the ideal number of children to be sampled per village is 10, then 25 households should be selected in each village, since 10 is 40% of 25. If there are several different units of interest within the households in a single survey, the number of households in each village should be chosen to include, on average, enough units of the rarest category.

Selecting the first house for the cluster

The ideal is to have a list of households in the village and choose a household at random from the list. This will be an acceptable procedure, even if the list is incomplete or out of date, and is certainly better than any other *ad hoc* procedure. If such a list is not available, an alternative is to find a point near the centre of the village and spin a bottle or similar object on the ground. Look in the direction indicated by the bottle when it comes to rest and judge roughly how many houses you might expect to pass if you walk in that direction until you reach the edge of the village. Suppose you think there might be about ten houses. Choose a random number between 1 and 10 and walk out in the indicated direction till you reach the corresponding house. The important principle is to avoid any method of choosing the first house that is likely to lead to the same kind of cluster in every village. For example, it would be an error to start always at the house of an important official. It may sometimes be socially necessary to interview such individuals. However, if the household would otherwise not have been selected, an abbreviated interview might be conducted simply to satisfy local protocol. The information obtained can be deleted later, before analysis begins, to avoid bias. Similarly, it would be an error always to choose the first house in the centre or at the edge of the village. It is not possible to make a formal rule that will be suitable in all cases. The use of common sense and knowledge of local conditions should lead to a sensible choice.

Selecting the remaining houses in the cluster

Again, local circumstances vary so much that it is not possible to define a universally appropriate method. The results of the survey will be more precise and representative if each cluster gives a wide coverage of the households and is not restricted to a small area around the first house. It is possible—that is, it would not invalidate the study—always to choose the nearest house to the previous one chosen, but it would be better to choose the second nearest, better still to choose the fifth nearest, and best of all to choose the households completely at random, if a dependable list or map is available.

Revisiting survey households when key informants are absent

It very often happens that the people needed for questioning in the households selected for the survey are not available when the survey team makes its visit, or that the household may be empty when visited. In such cases, arrangements should be made if possible to make repeated visits at a time when the missing people are most likely to be there. When the sampling unit is a household, arrangements may be made to use replacement households for those found to be empty. This could be done by having a pre-selected list of replacement households, to be drawn upon in a specified order. Such a list should only be used when the procedures for tracing the missing individuals from the households originally selected have been exhausted. Under no circumstances should interviewers be left to make decisions on the spot about what to do about the households with members missing.

4. The size of the sample

The precision of estimates made from the survey will depend on the size of the sample, the amount of clustering, and the item for which the value is being estimated. Other things being equal, the larger the sample, the more precise any estimates will be. However, for the same overall total sample size, a survey in which a large number of clusters is selected, with a few households in each, will give more precise results than one with a smaller number of clusters and a larger number of households in each. For example, a survey in which 300 mothers are interviewed will usually give more precise estimates than one in which 200 mothers are interviewed, but if the 300 are distributed as fifty clusters of six, they will give more precise estimates than if they were distributed as thirty clusters of ten.

On the other hand, it should be realized that a larger sample size and more clusters (even if somewhat smaller) will lead to an increased workload, which in turn means increases in cost and time. The resources available for a PHC review will be strictly limited, and usually this will mean a total sample size of a few hundred, spread over some tens of clusters.

Clustering affects the precision of any estimate from a survey, but the amount of this effect, known as the design effect, will be different for different items in the survey schedule.

The design effect (D) is given by:

$$D = 1 + (b - 1)r$$

where:

b = average number of responses received to this item per cluster, and

r = a measure of the correlation of responses to this item within the cluster, compared with the correlation in the population as a whole.

The value of r will be higher for items for which the value varies more between clusters. For example, socioeconomic items such as "husband's occupation—clerical or professional" will have a tendency to produce similar responses within a cluster, and will have r equal to about 0.10. On the other hand, demographic items such as "currently married" and morbidity and mortality measures such as "ill in past two weeks" will be no more likely to produce the same answer from two respondents in the same cluster than from two respondents in different clusters. These questions will have r very close to zero, i.e., approximately 0.01. In between these extremes will come questions related to health care practice and use of health care services. Responses to these questions will depend on the level of services locally and on local customs, and the value of r will probably be about 0.05.

As explained on p. 156 it is 95% certain that the interval:

(estimate $-$ 2SE) to (estimate $+$ 2SE)

will contain the true value. The design effect can be used to calculate the expected standard error for any given sample size and cluster size. The standard error is given by s, where:

$$s = \sqrt{p(1-p)D/n}$$

where:

    p = proportion expected to answer "yes" to item (note that this method can be used only for items that have a yes/no response),
    n = total number of responses to this item,
    D = design effect.

Thus

$$s = \sqrt{p(1-p)\,[1+(b-1)r]/n} \qquad\qquad \text{equation (1)}$$

Note that a guess has to be made at the proportion p even before the survey is carried out.

Table A3 gives some typical values of s for $r = 0.05$ (where c = number of clusters selected and b = the average number of responses received to the item, per cluster).

Suppose that a question of major interest is the immunization status of children aged 12–23 months, and that these children are expected to be found in 25% of households. If 30 clusters, each of 30 households, are taken, it would be expected that about 7 index children would be found in each cluster. If the immunization status is expected to be adequate for about 40% of these children, then $p = 0.4$ (40%), $c = 30$, $b = 7$, $r = 0.05$, and $n = 210$ (30×7), and, from the for-

Table A3. Expected standard error (s) (%) for different proportions (p) and clusters (c) and number of responses per cluster (b)

c	b	n ($c \times b$)	p (%) 50	40	20	15	10	5
50	4	200	3.79	3.71	3.03	2.71	2.27	1.37
40	5	200	3.87	3.79	3.10	2.77	2.32	1.69
30	7	210	3.93	3.85	3.15	2.81	2.36	1.31
20	10	200	4.26	4.17	3.41	3.04	2.55	1.86
50	60	3000	1.81	1.78	1.45	1.30	1.09	0.79
30	100	3000	2.23	2.18	1.78	1.59	1.34	0.97
15	200	3000	3.02	2.96	2.42	2.16	1.81	1.32

mula or from Table A3, the expected standard error is 0.0385, or 3.85%. It will be 95% certain that the true value of p lies within the range:

(estimate $-$ 7.7%) to (estimate $+$ 7.7%).

Suppose that the number of households to be selected in each village is h. It would be sensible to choose h to correspond to the number of households that can be dealt with comfortably in one day by one interviewing team, or a multiple of this number. This must, of course, take into account the time required for the random selection of houses, for walking between them, and for making up for non-response. The value of c will then be the number of clusters of size h that can easily be managed in the time available for the survey, and the total sample size is then $c \times h$.

The number of index individuals for any particular item of the schedule will be different for each village. The average value will be around b, but may turn out to be larger or smaller than this. The value of b itself will differ for different types of index; for example, in 20 households it may be expected to find 4 index children but 16 index mothers.

If it is known that a certain value of s is required from the survey, then the number of clusters needed can be calculated by:

$$c = p(1-p)\,[1 + (b-1)r]/(s^2 b) \qquad \text{equation (2)}$$

For example, suppose p is expected to be about 20% for some measure of disease prevalence, for which it can be expected that r will be about 0.01, and it is required that $s = 2.5\%$. The number of clusters required if each cluster contains 5 index individuals ($b = 5$), or 8 index individuals ($b = 8$), can be determined as follows:

Quantity	Calculation	Value for $b = 5$	Value for $b = 8$
A	$p(1-p)$	0.16	0.16
B	$1 + (b-1)r$	1.04	1.07
D	$A \times B$	0.1664	0.1712
E	$s^2 b$	0.0031	0.0050
C	D/E	54	34

Thus, either 54 clusters of 5 each, or 34 clusters of 8 each, would be expected to satisfy the requirements. If the index individuals are expected to be found in only about 50% of houses, then each cluster will need to contain 10 or 16 households, respectively.

Such calculations could be made for the most important responses in the survey. The number of clusters would then be the largest value of c given by equation (2).

Sometimes it may happen that the sample sizes needed for different items in the same survey will differ considerably. For example, a question on immunization may require a sample size of 200 children aged 12–23 months (or 800 households), whereas a question on diarrhoea morbidity may require a sample size of 1500 children aged 0–2 years (or 3000 households). In this case, the larger value of 3000 would be taken as the overall sample size to satisfy both criteria. However this would mean that about four times the information needed on immunization status would be collected. If sufficient resources are available, this will not be a problem, as it will give a more precise estimate, but, in practice, it may be more sensible to subsample for the immunization question. In other words, only every fourth index child aged 12–23 months found in the survey would be included in the sample. This will save time and effort, but adds to the complexity of the instructions given to interviewers, and so should be used with caution.

If the list of villages has been arranged in order according to some measure of PHC involvement, then there will be some improvement in precision, but this cannot be quantified adequately to allow its use in sample size calculations. The sample size should be calculated as if the list were unordered, with the benefit that the precision may, in fact, turn out to be better than that predicted.

If the survey has been explicitly stratified according to, for instance, ecological region, then each stratum should be considered as a separate survey and sample size calculations performed for each one to give the precision necessary for that region. The precision of the overall national estimate will then be somewhat better than that for any single region.

Should the survey be one of a series, and the purpose be to estimate the change in some measure since a previous review, then the 95% confidence interval for this change will be (estimated change − 2 SE) to (estimated change + 2 SE). In this case, the standard error is the standard error of the change, which will be larger than the standard error of the new estimate of the measure. This is because of the imprecision of the estimate of the measure from the previous survey. To allow for this, the sample size will need to be double that calculated by the usual methods.

If the comparison is to be made with a particular target figure chosen by the investigators, rather than one estimated from an earlier survey, then no extra imprecision is involved. The usual confidence interval of $\pm\, 2\,\mathrm{SE}$ still applies, and the sample size given by the usual calculations will be adequate.

5. Analysis of data

The most important goal of the analysis of the data is to provide estimates of important parameters, together with the standard errors of these estimates, so that confidence intervals can be calculated. It is possible to carry out all the necessary calculations without sophisticated equipment and the methods described below require only a calculator capable of calculating square roots. Whether a calculator or a microcomputer is used, the necessary calculations are often most clearly presented in the form of a spreadsheet.

There are commonly two different situations, each of which requires its own method of calculating estimates and standard errors. The choice of method is determined according to whether the desired estimate is obtained from a sample proportion or a sample ratio (see page 155). In addition, for each of these situations, if the sample was selected from an ordered list, different formulae are used to calculate the standard errors.

The use of simple spreadsheets for the calculation of estimates and the standard errors of these estimates is demonstrated using the example below. The sample sizes here are much smaller than those encountered in practice, but all the important steps in the calculations are demonstrated. For each type of situation, the basic calculations required for the sample estimate and its standard error are presented on pp. 166–175.

Survey example used for demonstration spreadsheets

Six villages are selected using a systematic pps procedure (see pages 157–158). Twenty households are chosen in each village to estimate, for the population:

● the proportion of households with latrines;

● the proportion of suitable index mothers who have received prenatal care.

The first will be estimated using the proportion of households in the sample with latrines.

The second is estimated using the ratio:

$$\frac{\text{Number of index mothers receiving prenatal care}}{\text{Number of index mothers in sample}}$$

Table A4. Data for survey example used for demonstration spreadsheets

Village	No. of households sampled in each village	No. of households with latrines	No. of index mothers in sampled households	No. of index mothers who received prenatal care
i	h_i	x_i	z_i	y_i
1	20	11	2	2
2	20	0	7	5
3	20	14	4	3
4	20	12	6	3
5	20	16	4	1
6	20	3	3	0

These data are shown in Table A4. The villages were arranged in order at the design stage of the survey according to the expected level of prenatal care. This fact is not taken into account in the analyses in sections *a–d* below, but is considered in sections *e* and *f*.

(a) Estimating a population proportion from a sample proportion
In the example, the sampling unit is the household and it is required to estimate the proportion of households that have a particular characteristic, in this case a latrine. For the general case, suppose that c villages have been selected and h households chosen in each village. The number of households in the i-th village that have a latrine can be denoted by x_i. The estimated proportion, p_i, of such households for the whole of this village is:

$$p_i = x_i/h$$

which is the proportion appearing in the sample. The estimate p of this proportion in the whole population is then the total number of households in the sample that have a latrine, divided by the total sample size, i.e.:

$$p = \Sigma x_i/n \qquad\qquad \text{equation (3)}$$

The sign Σ indicates that the terms should be summed over all values of i, thus:

$$\Sigma x_i = x_1 + x_2 + x_3 + \ldots + x_c$$

The required calculations are shown in Spreadsheet 1. For this example, p is equal to 0.4667, or 47% of sampled households.

Spreadsheet 1

Cluster data and calculations

Village i	No. of households with latrine x_i	x_i^2
1	11	121
2	0	0
3	14	196
4	12	144
5	16	256
6	3	9
	$A = 56$	$B = 726$

Sample size and sample proportion

Variable	Calculation	Definition	Value
c		No of villages in sample	6
h		No. of households sampled in each village	20
n	$c \times h$	No. of households in total sample	120
A	Σx_i	No. of households in sample with latrine	56
p	A/n	Proportion of households in sample with latrine	0.4667

Standard error calculations

New quantity	Calculation	Value
B	Σx_i^2	726
C	A^2	3136
D	C/c	522.67
E	$B - D$	203.33
F	$E/[c(c-1)]$	6.7777
G	$\sqrt{F}$	2.6034
$s(p)$	G/h	0.1302

*(b) Estimating the standard error of the estimate of
a population proportion*

The standard error of the proportion p, $s(p)$, is obtained by the formula:

$$s(p) = (1/h)\sqrt{\Sigma(p_i - p)^2/[c(c-1)]} \qquad \text{equation (4)}$$

For ease of calculation, this equation can also be expressed as:

$$s(p) = (1/h)\sqrt{[\Sigma x_i^2 - (\Sigma x_i)^2/c]/[c(c-1)]}$$

The last section of Spreadsheet 1 demonstrates the calculations required using the second form of equation 4. The resulting value of the standard error, $s(p)$, is 0.1302. The 95% confidence interval for the proportion of all households with a latrine is thus $0.4667 \pm 2 \times 0.1302$, i.e., 0.2063 to 0.7271 or between 21% and 73%. This interval is very wide because only 6 villages have been surveyed.

(c) Estimating a population ratio from a sample ratio

Suppose this time that h households have been selected in each of c villages with a view to estimating the proportion of suitably defined index individuals that have a particular characteristic. This might be the proportion of all children aged 1–2 years that has been fully immunized according to the criteria of the national immunization programme. Or it might be the proportion of all women who delivered a child during the previous 12 months who had at least 3 prenatal visits during the pregnancy, as is the case in the example used in Spreadsheet 2.

Let z_i be the number of index mothers in the sampled households in the i-th village and suppose that y_i of these mothers have had the specified number of prenatal visits. Then the proportion of the whole population of index mothers with this feature is estimated by:

$$R = \Sigma y_i / \Sigma z_i \qquad \text{equation (5)}$$

The calculation of the sample ratio R for the above example is shown in the middle section of Spreadsheet 2, where R is equal to 0.5385, or 54% of the index mothers in the sample.

Spreadsheet 2

Cluster data and calculations

Village i	No. of index mothers in sampled households who received prenatal care y_i	No. of index mothers in sampled households z_i	y_i^2	z_i^2	$y_i z_i$
1	2	2	4	4	4
2	5	7	25	49	35
3	3	4	9	16	12
4	3	6	9	36	18
5	1	4	1	16	4
6	0	3	0	9	0
	$A = 14$	$B = 26$	$C = 48$	$D = 130$	$E = 73$

Sample size and sample ratio

Variable	Calculation	Definition	Value
c		No. of villages in sample	6
A	Σy_i	No. of index mothers in sampled households who received prenatal care	14
B	Σz_i	No. of index mothers in sampled households	26
R	A/B	Sample ratio of index mothers who received prenatal care to total no. of index mothers in sample	0.5385

Standard error calculations

New quantity	Calculation	Value
R^2	R^2	0.2900
C	Σy_i^2	48
D	Σz_i^2	130
E	$\Sigma y_i z_i$	73
F	$2 \times R \times E$	78.621
G	$R^2 \times D$	37.7
H	$C - F + G$	7.079
J	$H/[c(c-1)]$	0.2360
K	$\sqrt{J}$	0.4858
$s(R)$	$c \times K/B$	0.1121

(d) Estimating the standard error of the estimate of a population ratio

The standard error of the estimate of the population ratio R, or $s(R)$, is:

$$s(R) = (c/\Sigma z_i)\sqrt{(\Sigma y_i^2 - 2R\Sigma y_i z_i + R^2\Sigma z_i^2)/[c(c-1)]} \qquad \text{equation (6)}$$

This more complicated formula for the standard error reflects the need to take into account the variation from village to village in the number of index mothers actually observed. The details of the calculations for the standard error of the ratio of index mothers receiving prenatal care in the example above are shown in the last section of Spreadsheet 2. In this example the standard error of the estimate, $s(R)$, is 0.1121.

The 95% confidence interval for the proportion of all index mothers receiving prenatal care is $0.5385 \pm 2 \times 0.1121$, i.e., 0.3143 to 0.7627 or between 31% and 76%.

(e) Estimating a population proportion and the standard error of the estimate from an ordered list

If the villages from which the sample was drawn were listed in order according to some criterion related to the measures being studied, the estimates would still be calculated in the same way, but the standard errors would be obtained from different formulae. The villages for the example were listed in order according to prior knowledge about the likely level of provision of prenatal care in each village. The use of an ordered list provides an implicit stratification, but only with respect to variables that are affected by the criterion used for ordering. The use of stratification should reduce the standard errors for the variables affected.

The example of a population proportion used on pp. 165–166 was the proportion of sample households with latrines. Since this variable is unlikely to be related to the expected level of prenatal care—the criterion used for ordering the list of villages—the standard error, calculated to take account of the ordering, would be expected to be similar to that obtained by the method used in Spreadsheet 1. In such a case it is better to calculate the standard error using the method in Spreadsheet 1 (or Spreadsheet 2 for the standard error of a population ratio). However, it would never be wrong to use the methods for ordered lists, even if the measure is unrelated to the ordering of the villages, though a slightly different answer would be obtained.

Spreadsheet 3 demonstrates the estimation of a population proportion and its standard error from an ordered list. The estimation of the proportion is the same as in Spreadsheet 1, $p = 56/120 = 0.4667$.

Spreadsheet 3

Cluster data and calculations

Village i	No. of households with latrine x_i	x_{i+1}	$x_i - x_{i+1}$	$(x_i - x_{i+1})^2$
1	11	0	11	121
2	0	14	− 14	196
3	14	12	2	4
4	12	16	− 4	16
5	16	3	13	169
6	3	—	—	—
	$A = 56$			$B = 506$

Sample size and sample proportion

Variable	Calculation	Definition	Value
c		No. of villages in sample	6
h		No. of households sampled in each village	20
A	Σx_i	No. of households in sample with latrine	56
p	$A/c \times h$	Proportion of households in sample with latrine	0.4667

Standard error calculations

New quantity	Calculation	Value
B	$\Sigma(x_i - x_{i+1})^2$	506
C	$(c \times B)/[2(c - 1)]$	303.6
D	$\sqrt{C}$	17.4241
$s(p)$	$D/(c \times h)$	0.1452

The standard error $s(p)$ for a proportion p obtained by sampling from an ordered list, is:

$$s(p) = (1/n) \sqrt{\{c/[2(c-1)]\} \sum_{i=1}^{c-1} (x_i - x_{i+1})^2} \qquad \text{equation (7)}$$

This formula is based on the differences between successive clusters, which would be expected to be smaller on an ordered list than if the clusters were in random order. Because of the paired comparisons seen in the cluster data calculations in Spreadsheet 3, there is no value of x_{i+1} for the last village.

Using the standard error calculations in Spreadsheet 3, $s(p) = 0.1452$. The 95% confidence interval for p is $0.4667 \pm 2 \times 0.1452$, i.e., 0.1763 to 0.7571. This is nearly the same as that given by Spreadsheet 1 (0.2063 to 0.7271), because the ordering with respect to prenatal care did not bear any relation to the availability of latrines. Thus there was no advantage in using this method of analysis for this question.

(f) Estimating a population ratio and the standard error of the estimate from an ordered list

As noted previously, the sample used as an example on p. 165 was drawn from villages listed in order according to the likely level of provision of prenatal care in each village. This procedure (see also pp. 157–158) is valid only if the villages are listed in order before the sample is chosen.

Spreadsheet 4 demonstrates the calculations required for the sample ratio and its standard error, using the same example as on pp. 168–169. The calculation of the sample ratio is identical to the procedure in Spreadsheet 2, and yields $R = 14/26 = 0.5385$.

The standard error $s(R)$ for a ratio R obtained from a sample drawn from an ordered list is:

$$s(R) = (1/\sum_{i=1}^{c} z_i)\sqrt{\{[c/2(c-1)][\sum_{i=1}^{c-1} (y_i - y_{i+1})^2}$$

$$- 2R \sum_{i=1}^{c-1} (y_i - y_{i+1})(z_i - z_{i+1}) + R^2 \sum_{i=1}^{c-1} (z_i - z_{i+1})^2]\}$$

$$\text{equation (8)}$$

As with equation (7), this formula is based on the differences between successive clusters, and there are no values of y_{i+1} or z_{i+1} for the last village.

Spreadsheet 4

Cluster data and calculations

Village i	No. of index mothers who received pre-natal care y_i	y_{i+1}	$y_i - y_{i+1}$	$(y_i - y_{i+1})^2$
1	2	5	− 3	9
2	5	3	2	4
3	3	3	0	0
4	3	1	2	4
5	1	0	1	1
6	0	—	—	—
	$A = 14$			$C = 18$

No. of index mothers in sampled households z_i	z_{i+1}	$z_i - z_{i+1}$	$(z_i - z_{i+1})^2$	$(y_i - y_{i+1})(z_i - z_{i+1})$
2	7	− 5	25	15
7	4	3	9	6
4	6	− 2	4	0
6	4	2	4	4
4	3	1	1	1
3	—	—	—	—
$B = 26$			$D = 43$	$E = 26$

Sample size and sample ratio

Variable	Calculation	Definition	Value
c		No. of villages in sample	6
A	Σy_i	No. of index mothers in sampled households who received prenatal care	14
B	Σz_i	No. of index mothers in sampled households	26
R	A/B	Sample ratio of mothers who received prenatal care to total no. of index mothers in sample	0.5385

Spreadsheet 4 (contd)		
Standard error calculations		
New quantity	Calculation	Value
R^2	R^2	0.2900
C	$\Sigma(y_i - y_{i+1})^2$	18
D	$\Sigma(z_i - z_{i+1})^2$	43
E	$\Sigma(y_i - y_{i+1})(z_i - z_{i+1})$	26
F	$2 \times R \times E$	28.002
G	$R^2 \times D$	12.47
H	$C - F + G$	2.468
J	$(c \times H)/[2(c - 1)]$	1.4808
K	$\sqrt{J}$	1.2169
$s(R)$	K/B	0.0468

On the basis of the calculations in Spreadsheet 4, $s(R) = 0.0468$. The 95% confidence interval for R is $0.5385 \pm 2 \times 0.0468$, i.e., 0.4449 to 0.6321. This interval is considerably narrower than the interval of 0.3143 to 0.7627 obtained from Spreadsheet 2. This demonstrates the substantial increase in precision that can be obtained by using an ordered list and the procedures demonstrated in Spreadsheets 3 and 4.

(g) Using the design effect to calculate standard errors
In order to save time in calculating the standard errors for all possible items and ratios of items in the questionnaire, many of them can be estimated approximately by using the achieved design effect for a few similar variables. The procedure is as follows:

(i) Estimate the values of p or R as appropriate for all the items of interest.

(ii) Calculate the standard error $s(p)$ or $s(R)$ for the most important items, as described above.

(iii) Estimate the design effect for these items (which may be different from the value assumed for the calculation of sample size) from:

$$D = (s^2(p)\,n)/(p(1 - p))$$

or

$$D = (s^2(R)\Sigma z_i)/(R(1 - R))$$

as appropriate.

(iv) For all other items, calculate the standard error as if the sample were a simple random sample, but multiply it by $\sqrt{D}$ to allow for clustering, where D is the design effect for an item in the questionnaire that is expected to have a similar distribution. Thus:

$$s(p) = \sqrt{p(1-p)D/n}$$

and

$$s(R) = \sqrt{R(1-R)D/\Sigma z_i}$$

Using this approach, p and R are calculated for all items, but the calculation of s, as shown in Spreadsheets 1–4, is needed for only a few items.

6. Multistage samples

The method described in the previous sections can easily be generalized to more complex designs provided that a few conditions are satisfied. These are best demonstrated by examples.

Two-stage sampling

Suppose a country is divided into districts, a sample of districts is chosen and then a sample of villages within each chosen district. The districts should be chosen exactly as described on pp. 157–158, by the systematic pps method. That is, there must be some measure of the population size of each district, the districts must be listed, the cumulative population size calculated, and so on. (Again it will be beneficial to list the districts in order according to the expected values of some important measure being studied in the survey, if this is possible.) Within each district, villages are selected, again by the systematic pps method, the same number of villages being selected in every district.

The decision on the sample size and the structure of the sample can be made exactly as described on pp. 160–165, except that h will now be the number of households per district, b will be the expected number of index individuals per district, and c will be the number of districts in the sample. The value of r is now an approximate measure of the correlation of responses within the district.

The analysis will also follow exactly the same pattern as in section 5 and Spreadsheets 1–4, except that x_i will now be the number of houses in the i-th district that have a latrine, z_i will be the number of index mothers sampled in this district, and y_i will be the number of them who received prenatal care.

A special case can arise with pps sampling, when a district has a population that is larger than the sampling interval. In this case it may be selected twice and care is needed. An example will make the situation clear. Suppose 3 districts are to be selected from 5 districts with populations as follows:

District	Population	Cumulative population
A	10 000	10 000
B	5 000	15 000
C	25 000	40 000
D	8 000	48 000
E	6 000	54 000

In this case, the sampling interval will be $54\,000/3 = 18\,000$. Begin by choosing a random number between 1 and 18 000. If the random number is 6320, then the key values will be 6320, 24 320, 42 320 and districts A, C and D will be chosen. If the random number is 1018, the key values will be 1018, 19 018 and 37 018 so that the chosen districts will be A, C, and C again. To save confusion, call them A, C1, and C2. Note that it would be incorrect to ignore this repetition and choose another district instead of C for the third sample. The three districts, A, C1 and C2, should then be subsampled, just as though they were all different. In other words, two independent samples of clusters will be selected in district C. The analysis is then carried out, just as if three distinct districts had been chosen.

More than two stages of sampling

Suppose that there are too many districts to be sampled directly. Then it is possible to take a sample of regions, a sample of districts within these regions, and a sample of villages within these districts. Provided that regions, districts, and villages are all chosen using pps, that the same number of districts is chosen in every region, and that the same number of villages is chosen in every district, then all the remarks above apply if the word "district" is replaced by the word "region".

7. Stratified samples

Suppose that a country is divided into a number of regions, on an administrative, ecological, or other basis. A stratified sample can then be obtained by selecting samples independently from each of the regions. Decisions about the size and structure of the samples should be made separately for each region and the samples can be of a different type and/or size for each region.

An estimate for each region should then be calculated together with its standard error. Suppose there are 3 regions and that the estimates for the regions are p_1, p_2 and p_3, with standard errors s_1, s_2 and s_3, respectively. Then the estimate for the whole country would be:

$$p = w_1 p_1 + w_2 p_2 + w_3 p_3$$

with standard error

$$s(p) = \sqrt{w_1^2 s_1^2 + w_2^2 s_2^2 + w_3^2 s_3^2}$$

where w_1 is the proportion of the country's population that belongs to region 1, and so on (of course, $w_1 + w_2 + w_3 = 1$).

Stratified samples may be used even when not all the regions in the country are chosen. This will occur when regions are selected purposively. In this case, the survey cannot be representative of the country as a whole. However, it can be considered that the regions actually chosen are the "country" of interest in the survey and that the sample can be considered as a stratified sample of this "pseudo-country" to which the results can be generalized.

8. Presentation of results

A primary health care review provides an opportunity to gather up-to-date information, in the field, on variables that are likely to be of interest to professionals of many kinds. It is difficult to imagine, at the moment of compiling a report, all the different purposes for which the survey data might eventually be of use. It is therefore advisable to describe these data as fully as possible and, at the very least, to provide tables for all the important variables at the cluster level. For example, if information has been collected about the vaccination status of index children, a table should appear showing clearly, for each cluster, the number of households selected, the number of index children in those households, and how many of the children had been fully vaccinated. It is not necessary to place these detailed tables in the main text of the report, but they should, at least, be presented in an appendix.

Tables should be well laid out. The numbers in tables should be carefully aligned with a clear border of white space around each number so that it can be read easily. There is no value in specifying the numbers too precisely; this actually makes them harder to assimilate. If percentages are being quoted, it is never worth giving more than one decimal place. Unless some of the percentages are very small—1% or 2%—they should all be quoted to the nearest whole number. Standard errors should be quoted to the same degree of accuracy as the estimates.

Pictorial presentation of results using bar charts, histograms, pie-charts, etc. is a great aid to rapid assimilation of the main features of the data and gives extra life to the report. The data on which the representations are based should be included in an appendix. Key figures pertinent to the analysis may be mentioned in the text, but good diagrams often indicate trends, relationships, and comparisons much more clearly than the figures themselves.

9. General principles of sample design

- Units at all levels, except the lowest level (households), should be selected with probability proportional to size.

- Households should be selected by simple random sampling, as far as possible.

- As many higher-level units (districts or villages) should be selected as resources will allow. At any level, many small clusters will give better results than a few large clusters.

- At all levels, the same number of units should be sampled within each higher-level unit, i.e., the same number of districts in every region, the same number of villages in every district, and the same number of households in every village.

- At any level, it will be better if units can be listed in order according to some criterion related to the subject of the survey, or to some general measure of PHC involvement.

- Stratification can be used only at the top level (region or province). In this case, each region or province should be considered as a separate survey.

- Different sample designs can be used in different strata. This may be useful if the country consists of a few very different regions. The results can then be combined at the end of the survey.

- If estimates are needed for regions, then sample size calculations should be performed for each region. The combined estimate for the whole country will then be more precise than the regional estimates.

- At least two top-level units (e.g., districts) must always be chosen within each stratum, to allow calculation of standard errors.

- Districts or regions may be chosen purposively rather than at random if they are of particular interest in themselves. The results for such districts are then valid for the districts in question, but cannot be combined to give a representative national result.

- Areas of the country that cannot be surveyed economically may be omitted from the sample design; the results should then be presented for the country excluding these areas.

- If you wish to go beyond these guidelines, then a statistician experienced in survey sampling methods should be consulted.

Traditional birth attendant (TBA)

Date of interview. . . . .
Name of interviewer. . . . . .

1. Personal details
1.1 Name . . . .
1.2 Community . . . . .District. . . . .
1.3 Supervisory health centre/facility . . . .

(Tick answer given)

1.4 Distance to health centre/facility	under 1 km (under 15 min)	. . . .
	1–4 km (15 min–1 h)	. . . .
	5–10 km (1–2 h)	. . . .
	over 10 km (>2 h)	. . . .
	don't know	. . . .
1.5 Age	under 20 years	. . . .
	20–29 years	. . . .
	30–39 years	. . . .
	40–49 years	. . . .
	50 years or over	. . . .
	don't know	. . . .
1.6 Sex	male	. . . .
	female	. . . .
1.7 Marital status	single	. . . .
	married	. . . .
	widow/widower	. . . .
	divorced	. . . .
	separated	. . . .
	no answer	. . . .
1.8 No. of TBA's children	none	. . . .
	1–3	. . . .
	more than 3	. . . .
1.9 Place of birth of TBA	within area of work	. . . .
	outside but near area	. . . .
	far from area of work	. . . .

1.10 Time the TBA has lived   all life   . . . .
     within area of work   5 years or more   . . . .
                                  less than 5 years   . . . .

1.11 Previous or usual
     occupation (other than TBA
     work)   . . . .

1.12 Can the TBA read?   Yes . . . .
     (*Show simple text in appro-*   No . . . .
     priate language and
     script)

1.13 Level of formal education   none   . . . .
                                 primary   . . . . . .
                                 secondary   . . . . . .
                                 technical   . . . . . .
                                 other (*specify*) . . . .

2. Community information

2.1 Find out from the TBA if she has information on the following
    regarding the people in her community:

		TBA response	Actual number	Source
(*a*)	Total population of community	. . . .	. . . . .	. . . .
(*b*)	Total number of households	. . . .	. . . . .	. . . .
(*c*)	Number of births per year	. . . .	. . . . .	. . . .
(*d*)	Total number of pregnancies	. . . .	. . . . .	. . . .
(*e*)	Average birth interval	. . . .	. . . . .	. . . .
(*f*)	Number of children under 1 year of age	. . . .	. . . . .	. . . .

2.2 What does the TBA say are the causes of maternal death in her
    area? . . . .

2.3 What does the TBA say are the most common causes of infant
    death in her area? . . . .

2.4 What practices and taboos on food and hygiene does the TBA say
    are commonly observed within the community?
    (*a*) during pregnancy . . . .
    (*b*) during labour . . . .
    (*c*) after delivery . . . .

3. Selection and training of TBAs

3.1 Was the TBA selected by the community
for the post of TBA?

Yes. . . . .
No . . . . .

If yes, how was she selected?   (*Tick answer given*)

    by a meeting of the whole community   . . . . .
    by a committee of the community   . . . . .
    by a women's group   . . . . .
    by community leaders   . . . . .
    other (*specify*) . . . .

3.2 For how long has she been working as a TBA?
    0–4 years   . . . . .
    5–9 years   . . . . .
    10–19 years   . . . . .
    20–29 years   . . . . .
    30 years or more   . . . . .
    don't know   . . . . .

3.3 From whom did the TBA originally learn her skills?
    no training   . . . . .
    from mother   . . . . .
    from other relative   . . . . .
    from other TBA   . . . . .
    from health facility personnel   . . . . .
    other (*specify*) . . . .

3.4 Did the TBA receive a basic training
course from the health facility?

Yes. . . . .
No . . . . .

If yes, how long was the course?. . . . . . . .weeks/months
(*Interviewer should compare this with national guidelines.*)

3.5 Does her work include anything for which
she has had insufficient or no training?

Yes. . . . .
No . . . . .

If yes, specify . . . .

3.6 Has the TBA participated in a refresher
training course in the past 12 months?

Yes. . . . .
No . . . . .

If yes, what was the latest course about? . . . .

3.7 In which areas or skills does she feel that
further training is necessary?
    (*a*). . . . .
    (*b*). . . . .
    (*c*). . . . .
    No need for further training   . . . . .
    Don't know   . . . . .

4.   Support, supervision and working conditions

4.1   Has the TBA ever been visited by   Yes. . . . .
anybody from the health facility?   No . . . . .
If yes, by whom?. . . . .
How long ago was the last visit?   . . . . .
less than 1 month   . . . . .
1–3 months   . . . . .
more than 3 months   . . . . .
What was the purpose of this visit?
supply   . . . . .
supervision   . . . . .
training   . . . . .
other (*specify*). . . . .
don't know   . . . . .

4.2   Has the TBA recently visited her   Yes. . . . .
referral health facility?   No . . . . .
If yes, how long ago was the latest visit?
less than 1 month
1–3 months   . . . . .
more than 3 months   . . . . .
What was the purpose of this latest visit?
supplies   . . . . .
patient referral   . . . . .
advice   . . . . .
submit report   . . . . .
meeting   . . . . .
training   . . . . .
other (*specify*). . . . .

4.3   How many deliveries has the TBA conducted in the past month?
Number of deliveries: none   . . . . .
1   . . . . .
2–3   . . . . .
more than 3   . . . . .
don't know   . . . . .
In the past 3 months?
Number of deliveries: none   . . . . .
1–5   . . . . .
6–10   . . . . .
more than 10   . . . . .
don't know   . . . . .

4.4   Were any of the deliveries she conducted   Yes. . . . .
attended by her supervisor?   No . . . . .

4.5 Does the TBA receive any form   Yes. . . . .
of remuneration or reward?   No . . . . .
If yes, specify in what form (e.g., certificate, money, goods) . . . .
From whom?. . . . .

4.6 Does the TBA have a special place assigned   Yes. . . . .
by the community for her work?   No . . . . .

4.7 How many patients has the TBA referred to a health facility
in the past 3 months?
Number of referrals: none   . . . . .
                     1–3   . . . . .
                     more than 3   . . . . .
                     don't know   . . . . .

4.8 Did the community arrange transport   Yes. . . . .
for the referrals?   No . . . . .
If yes, specify . . . .

4.9 In what other ways does the community help in her work?
(*If none, say so*). . . . .

5. Routine activities

5.1 General activities
What activities does the TBA carry out? (*Tick as answered–
do not prompt.*)
     Prenatal care   . . . . .
     Conduct of labour   . . . . .
     Postnatal care   . . . . .
     Referral of difficult cases   . . . . .
     Prenatal screening for risks   . . . . .
     Home visiting   . . . . .
     Health education   . . . . .
     MCH clinic   . . . . .
     Immunizations   . . . . .
     Child growth monitoring   . . . . .
     Oral rehydration   . . . . .
     Malaria prophylaxis   . . . . .
     Treatment of common illnesses   . . . . .
     Female circumcision   . . . . .
     Birth registration   . . . . .
     Other (*specify*). . . . .

5.2 Prenatal care
     (i) Do pregnant women in her area   Yes. . . . .
          register for prenatal care?   No . . . . .
                                         Don't know. . . . .

If yes, where do they register? . . . .

How many register?   few   . . . . .

                                               about half   . . . . .

                                               nearly all   . . . . .

                                               don't know   . . . . .

(ii)   What specific action does the TBA take when she
        knows of a pregnant woman who has failed to regis-
        ter for prenatal care? (*Tick answer given—do not
        prompt*)

        Sends for her   . . . . .

        Counsels her   . . . . .

        Visits her home   . . . . .

        None   . . . . .

        Other (*specify*). . . . .

(iii)   Does the TBA refer every pregnant woman to the
        health facility for a routine prenatal check-up?

                                                  Yes . . . . .

                                                  No . . . . .

        If yes, is she informed of the results   Yes . . . . .

        of the visit?   No . . . . .

(iv)   What activities does the TBA carry out during a
        routine prenatal visit?

        . . . .

        . . . .

        . . . .

(v)   Which of the following categories of pregnant moth-
        ers would she routinely look after herself and which
        would she always refer for prenatal care at the
        hospital or health centre? (*Tick answers given—do
        not prompt*)

Client category[a]	Cared for by TBA	Referred to hospital/ health centre
Healthy mother in 3rd or later pregnancy	. . . .	. . . .
Mother less than 16 years old	. . . .	. . . .
Mother older than 45 years in 1st pregnancy	. . . .	. . . .

[a] Select items according to prevailing national guidelines.

Previous caesarean	. . . .	. . . .
Mother with short stature	. . . .	. . . .
Mother with severe limp	. . . .	. . . .
Previous delivery with forceps	. . . .	. . . .
Bleeding in present pregnancy	. . . .	. . . .
Previous retained placenta	. . . .	. . . .
Previous stillbirth or neonatal death	. . . .	. . . .
Previous period of subfertility	. . . .	. . . .
Mother with serious medical illness	. . . .	. . . .
Malnourished mother	. . . .	. . . .
Multiple pregnancy (twins, triplets)	. . . .	. . . .
Serious bleeding after previous delivery	. . . .	. . . .

(vi) What does the TBA do about the following conditions? (Review team should make a list of a few of these complications relevant to country situation.) (*Ask one by one— indicate if answer is "don't know"*)

Prenatal complications[a]	Action suggested by TBA
Bleeding in early pregnancy	. . . .
Bleeding in late pregnancy	. . . .
Severe/prolonged vomiting	. . . .
Severe abdominal pain	. . . .
Frequent and painful urination	. . . .
Swelling of hands and feet	. . . .
Severe headaches	. . . .
Failure to gain weight	. . . .
Failure of womb to grow	. . . .
Tense and tender abdomen	. . . .
Severe shortness of breath	. . . .
Early labour cramps	. . . .
Leakage of liquid	. . . .
No movement in womb	. . . .
High fever	. . . .

[a] The following may be added if the TBA has been taught how to recognize them: severe anaemia, jaundice, hypertension.

5.3 Labour and delivery

   (i) Does the TBA practise any methods to attempt to   Yes. . .
speed up delivery? (*N.B. This question is aimed*   No . . .
*at detecting persistence of potentially harmful
practices.*)
If yes, specify. . . . .

  (ii) What does the TBA normally do when the following
complications develop during the conduct of labour?
(*Ask one by one—indicate if answer is "don't know"*)

Labour complication[a]	Action suggested by TBA
Heavy bleeding from vagina	. . . .
Abdomen hard and tender	. . . .
Bulging forewaters	. . . .
Cord prolapses	. . . .
Arm or leg presenting	. . . .
Breech presentation	. . . .
Multiple pregnancy suspected	. . . .
Contractions fading	. . . .
Labour becomes prolonged	. . . .
Fluid becomes foul	. . . .
Mother has a fit	. . . .
Shoulder gets stuck	. . . .
Tight circumcision scar	. . . .
Severe perineal tear	. . . .
Cord tightly round baby's neck	. . . .

5.4 Third stage of labour

   (i) At which stage does the TBA normally cut the
umbilical cord? (*Tick answer given—do not prompt*)
     Immediately the baby is born   . . . . .
     When cord ceases to pulsate   . . . . .
     When placenta delivered   . . . . .
     Other (*specify*). . . . .

  (ii) How does the TBA recognize that the placenta has
separated? (*Tick answer given—do not prompt*)

[a] Select items in accordance with the national situation.

      Fundus gets hard and rises   . . . . .

      Small loss of blood   . . . . .

      Cord stump lengthens   . . . . .

      Woman has urge to push   . . . . .

      Afterbirth visible   . . . . .

      Other (*specify*). . . . .

(iii) How does the TBA normally deliver the placenta? . . . .

    . . . .

(iv) If a mother is bleeding after delivery, what does the
     TBA do? . . . .

 (v) How many mothers died in the past 3 months
     because of bleeding after delivery?

      One   . . . . .

      More than one   . . . . .

(vi) How many mothers died in the past 3 months because
     of fever after delivery?

      One   . . . . .

      More than one   . . . . .

5.5 Care of the newborn

  (i) What does the TBA do when a child fails to breathe or
     stops breathing soon after birth? (*Tick answer
     given—do not prompt*)

      Wipes out excess fluid and mucus from mouth and
       nostrils   . . . . .

      Holds baby upside down and smacks bottom   . . . . .

      Gives mouth-to-mouth resuscitation   . . . . .

      Other (*specify*) . . . .

      Nothing   . . . . .

 (ii) How does the TBA ensure that the baby is kept warm
     after birth? (*Tick answer given—do not prompt*)

      Dries baby with a clean towel   . . . . .

      Wraps baby in warm linen   . . . . .

      Lets mother cuddle infant   . . . . .

      Avoids washing baby for the first day   . . . . .

      Washes baby with warm water   . . . . .

      Other (*specify*) . . . .

      Don't know   . . . . .

(iii) What would make the TBA suspect that something
     was wrong with the cord stump? (*Tick answer
     given—do not prompt*)

      Bleeding from cord   . . . . .

      Foul smell   . . . . .

Foul discharge . . . . .
Stump moist . . . . .
Delayed separation of placenta . . . . .
Other (*specify*). . . . .
Don't know . . . . .

(iv) Does the TBA do anything to the infant's eyes soon
after delivery? (*Tick answer given–do not prompt*)
Wipes clean . . . . .
Applies medicine (*specify*) . . . . .
Other (*specify*). . . . .
Nothing . . . . .

(v) Does the TBA ensure that mother and   Yes . . . . .
child register with the MCH clinic?   No . . . . .

5.6 MCH/FP/EPI/health education
(*Select questions only when national TBA programme includes
these activities*)

(i) Does the TBA participate regularly in the   Yes . . . . .
MCH clinic that serves her community?   No . . . . .
If no, why not?
TBA not invited . . . . .
The clinic is too far away . . . . .
Other (*specify*). . . . .
Don't know . . . . .

(ii) How often are immunization services available in her
area? . . . . .
Daily . . . . .
Weekly . . . . .
Monthly . . . . .
Every 2 months . . . . .
Other (*specify*). . . . .
Not available . . . . .
Don't know . . . . .

(iii) What specific functions does she perform on a regular
basis within the immunization programme? (*Tick
answer given—do not prompt*) . . . . . .
Community motivation . . . . .
Generally assist at sessions . . . . .
Follow up defaulters . . . . .
No active part at all . . . . .
Other (*specify*). . . . .

(iv) Does she have any health information   Yes . . . . .
materials to hand out to the community?   No . . . . .

If yes, specify what information she has given in the
past 3 months . . . .

5.7 Nutrition and diarrhoea control
   (i)   Does the TBA weigh the children herself? Yes . . . . .
                                                   No   . . . . .
         If yes, is her scale accurate?   Yes . . . . .
         (*Do physical check*)   No   . . . . .
   (ii) Does the TBA understand the growth chart used in
         this area?
         She says that she:
             knows and understands the growth chart[a]   . . . . .
             knows but does not understand the growth chart . . . .
             does not know the growth chart   . . . . .
         Interviewer assessment:
             TBA understands growth chart   . . . . .
             TBA does not understand growth chart   . . . . .
   (iii) Up to what age does the TBA believe that mothers
         should breast-feed their babies? (*Tick answer given—
         do not prompt*)
             Less than 3 months   . . . . .
             3 months   . . . . .
             6 months   . . . . .
             12 months   . . . . .
             24 months   . . . . .
             Other (*specify*) . . . .
             Don't know   . . . . .
   (iv) How does the TBA recognize dehydration in a young
         child? (*Tick answer given—do not prompt*)
             Dry mouth   . . . . .
             Severe thirst   . . . . .
             Sunken eyes   . . . . .
             Sunken fontanelle   . . . . .
             Loss of skin elasticity   . . . . .
             Little or no tears or urine   . . . . .
             Weak pulse   . . . . .
             General weakness and collapse   . . . . .
             Other (*specify*) . . . .
             Don't know   . . . . .

---

[a] If this answer has been ticked, the interviewer should assess, by further questioning, whether the TBA
really understands the growth chart.

(v) Does the TBA know how to prepare a sugar Yes . . . . .
and salt solution for treatment of diarrhoea? No . . . . .
If yes, describe . . . .
Interviewer assessment:
this agrees with local official formula Yes . . . . .
No . . . . .

(vi) What advice does the TBA give to a mother whose child
has diarrhoea? (*Tick answer given—do not prompt*)
    Continue with breast-feeding . . . . .
    Stop breast-feeding* . . . . .
    Give extra fluids . . . . .
    Give ORS solution or sugar and salt solution . . . . .
    Give medicaments** (*specify*). . . . .
    Continue to feed child normally . . . . .
    Feed child more frequently . . . . .
    Stop solid feeding* . . . . .
    Watch for signs of dehydration . . . . .
    Seek help if child not improving with sugar and
      salt solution . . . . .
    Explain how to prevent diarrhoea in future . . . . .
    Other (*specify*). . . . .
    Don't know . . . . .

6. Supplies and equipment

6.1 Does the TBA have a list of the drugs and Yes . . . . .
equipment that she should have? No . . . . .

6.2 What is the arrangement for replenishing supplies?
. . . .

6.3 Did she run out of supplies of any Yes . . . . .
items in the past 3 months? No . . . . .
If yes, which items have been out of stock during the past 3
months and what were the reasons for the shortage?

Items	Reasons
. . . .	. . . .
. . . .	. . . .
. . . .	. . . .

* Example of incorrect answer.
** Check with national policy.

6.4 Drug supply

Item[a]	Current stock	Date of last supply	Date next supply due
Aspirin			
Chloroquine			
ORS			
Condoms			
etc.			

[a] Select items according to national standard (e.g., iron tablets, ergometrine tablets, eye ointment, silver nitrate drops, contraceptive pills, IUDs).

6.5 Equipment and other supplies

Item[a]	Present (+) or absent (0)	Condition (good = + poor = 0)	Other comments
Apron			
Forceps			
Cotton wool			
Towels			
etc.			

[a] Select items according to national standard (e.g., adult weighing scale, infant weighing scale, scissors/razor blades, cord ligature, sterilizing equipment, lamp or torch, record forms, pen/pencil, paper, etc.).

Community leaders

Date of interview . . . .
Name of interviewer . . . .

Name of community . . . .
Name of community leader interviewed . . . .
Function . . . .

1. Community organization

1.1 Is there a village committee or similar mechanism   Yes   . . . . .
for collective decision-making on the community's   No   . . . . .
health and health-related affairs?
If yes, who are the members (by categories of
people and groups they represent)? . . . .
If no, how are decisions taken? . . . .
If the answer is "no", go to 2.

1.2 Is this committee statutory (established in   Yes   . . . . .
accordance with the law of the country)?   No   . . . . .

1.3 Does any health worker attend this committee?   Yes   . . . . .
                                                       No   . . . . .

If yes, what is his or her status on the committee
(e.g., chairman, secretary, treasurer, member,
invited advisor, consultant)? . . . .

1.4 Is this committee part of a larger village committee Yes   . . . . .
responsible for overall socioeconomic development   No   . . . . .
and other affairs (multisectoral functions)?
If no, what other village committees exist? . . . .
. . . .

1.5 What are the functions of the committee that deals
with community health? (*Tick as answered—do not
prompt*)
Deciding on priorities for local health action   . . . . .
Mobilizing local resources for health activities (e.g.,
   planning and implementing communal economic
   activities to support PHC)   . . . . .
Obtaining outside resources for local health
   activities   . . . . .

Planning and implementing (PHC) health and
health-related activities   . . . . .

Employing community health workers   . . . . .

Supervising the nontechnical aspects of the work of
the CHW   . . . . .

Dealing with emergency health situations (e.g.,
arranging for transportation of emergency medical
referrals from the village)   . . . . .

Other (*specify*) . . . .

1.6 How long ago did the committee last meet?

         Less than 1 month   . . . . .

         1–3 months   . . . . .

         More than 3 months   . . . . .

What was discussed? . . . .

1.7 Are minutes of the committee's meetings available? Yes . . . . .
(*Team should ask to see an example.*)   No   . . . . .

1.8 Does the committee keep accounts of its   Yes . . . . .
finances?   No   . . . . .
If yes, are they audited?   Yes . . . . .
(*Team should ask to see an example.*)   No   . . . . .

2. Perception of health problems and health services

2.1 What does the leader regard as the main health
problems in the community?. . . . .

2.2 What does the leader feel are the main causes of
these problems? . . . .

2.3 Who are most affected?. . . . .
Does the leader know these people personally?   Yes . . . . .
                                                     No   . . . . .

2.4 What does the leader think the community should
do about these problems, especially the ones that
cause most suffering? . . . .

2.5 What has already been done?. . . . .

2.6 Does the community consider that the health   Yes . . . . .
programme has helped to reduce the community's No   . . . . .
health problems?

2.7 What information does the community collect on the health situation (e.g., immunization, births, measles incidence, latrines, food supplies)?................
....

2.8 How many people have died in the past month?............

2.9 Which of the following local health services are being provided? Is the community leader satisfied with them? (*Tick as answered—ask one by one*)

	Provided and satisfactory	Provided but unsatisfactory	Not provided
Curative health services	....		
Maternal and child health services	....		
Environmental health services	....		
Health education	....		
Nutrition education and promotion	....		
Family planning	....		
Immunization	....		
Control of specific diseases	....		

For each service with which the leader is not satisfied, give reasons...............................
....

3. Community resources and self-reliance

3.1 Can the community raise funds (local taxes)?   Yes .....
                                                 No .....
If yes, what does the community use the money for?..........
....

3.2 In the last 2 years, has the community requested   Yes .....
and received, directly or indirectly, any external   No .....
health aid (in cash or in kind)?
If yes, specify what for, how much, and where the aid came from...

3.3 Enumerate communal health activities carried out during the past 12 months. (*Tick as answered— do not prompt*)

Water supply . . . . .
Sanitation/excreta disposal . . . . .
Village cleanliness/solid waste disposal . . . . .
Transport of sick . . . . .
Promotion of nutrition . . . . .
Communal farming for health support . . . . .
Other (*specify*):. . . . .

3.4 Are there any health projects (ongoing or   Yes . . . . .
proposed) planned by the community itself? No . . . . .
If yes, is government or external support needed?. . . . .
Describe the project(s) and the type and quantity
of assistance required. . . . .

3.5 Has the community developed or acquired any
new income-generating activities over the past Yes . . . . .
2 years? No . . . . .
If yes, specify . . . .

3.6 Has the prosperity of the community generally Yes . . . . .
improved in recent years? No . . . . .
If yes, describe some examples of progress . . . .
. . . .

4. Community health workers

4.1 Is the community satisfied with the work and
behaviour of the:
community health worker(s)? Yes . . . . .
  No . . . . .
  NA[a] . . . . .
traditional birth attendant(s)? Yes . . . . .
  No . . . . .
  NA[a] . . . . .
If no, specify dissatisfaction . . . .
. . . .

4.2 Has it been necessary during the last two
years to remove or replace any of the:
community health workers? Yes . . . . .
  No . . . . .
  NA[a] . . . . .
traditional birth attendants? Yes . . . . .
  No . . . . .
  NA[a] . . . . .
If yes, specify . . . .

---

[a] NA = not applicable (for example, where there is no CHW/TBA).

4.3 Do the CHWs and TBAs report to the committee about the following:

		CHW	TBA
(a) Problems encountered (that need action)	Yes	. . . . . .	. . . . .
	No	. . . . . .	. . . . .
(b) Proposals and plans for required health activities	Yes	. . . . . .	. . . . .
	No	. . . . . .	. . . . .
(c) Progress of their work in general	Yes	. . . . . .	. . . . .
	No	. . . . . .	. . . . .

4.4 If health workers submit reports, how many times did the committee meet to discuss such reports over the past 12 months?

                                                       Never . . . .
                                                       Twice . . . .
     More than twice . . . .

4.5 What remuneration or reward does the community/committee provide for its community health workers (e.g., regular payment in cash, remuneration in kind, certificate, uniform, exemption from other community duties)?

. . . .

4.6 Has the community/committee managed to provide the remuneration without fail in the past 12 months?

          Yes . . . . . .
          No . . . . . .

4.7 What other services/support are given to CHWs/TBAs? . . . .

. . . .

4.8 Have any complaints been received from CHWs/TBAs in the last 12 months?

          Yes . . . . . .
          No . . . . . .

If yes, describe the complaints . . . .

. . . .

5. Contribution of other sectors to health

5.1 Are there other persons in the community who are involved in promoting community health and well-being (e.g., schoolteachers, agricultural workers, religious leaders)?

          Yes . . . . . .
          No . . . . . .

5.2 If yes, who are they? . . . .

. . . .

Give specific examples of what they do . . . .
Are these activities coordinated with those of the health worker(s)?

          Yes . . . . . .
          No . . . . . .

If yes, specify . . . .

5.3 Does the community have community workers in   Yes . . . . . .
    other sectors (such as agriculture, development,   No . . . . . .
    religion)?
    If yes, who are they?. . . . .

5.4 Does the community have access to a rural/bank   Yes . . . . . .
    credit scheme?   No . . . . . .
    If yes, what do these credits cover?. . . . .
    . . . .

5.5 Does the community have a supplementary   Yes . . . . . .
    feeding programme?   No . . . . . .
    If yes, specify . . . .

5.6 Does the community have subsidized seeds,   Yes . . . . . .
    fertilizers, foods?   No . . . . . .
    If yes, specify . . . .
    . . . .

5.7 Do the people have to go far for water   Yes . . . . . .
    (if this is applicable)?   No . . . . . .
    If yes, specify . . . .

5.8 Do you know of any plans for roads that are   Yes . . . . . .
    going to be built?   No . . . . . .
    If yes, specify . . . .

5.9 Do different sectors' activities in the community   Yes . . . . . .
    compete, conflict or overlap with each other?   No . . . . . .
    If yes, give one example . . . .

5.10 Are any projects contributing to ill health   Yes . . . . . .
    in your area, e.g., irrigation, resettlement,   No . . . . . .
    deforestation?
    If yes, give examples. . . . .

5.11 Are there cooperatives?   Yes . . . . . .
        No . . . . . .

    If yes, specify . . . .
    Do they work well?   Yes . . . . . .
        No . . . . . .

Questionnaires

Form A: Household questionnaire

Note: this part of the sample questionnaire is in the form of a checklist; no numbers or written answers should be put down. There are 10 columns to tick (check), corresponding to the answers from 10 households. On the top line, the interviewer should fill in the sequence number of the household. One column should be completed at each house visited. When the form is full, the interviewer should start a new form until the required total number of households per cluster has been visited. Space is available on the back of the form to add any necessary written details.

It is advisable to shade all areas where there are no answers to be ticked.

The footnotes are listed on p. 213.

HOUSEHOLD QUESTIONNAIRE

Number of cluster _____   Name of village _____
Date _____   Name of district _____

	1	2	3	4	5	6	7	8	9	10	Total	Code
Sequence no. of household in the cluster												
1. Respondent **(Tick one)** **(The mother should always be the respondent if possible)**												
Mother												1
Other (*specify overleaf*)												2
2. Has the household been visited by a CHW within the last 4 weeks? **(Tick one)**												
Yes												1
No												2
No CHW in the area												3
Don't know or no response												9
3. Has the CHW given you advice on sanitation or cleanliness?[a] **(Tick one)**												
Yes												1
No												2
No CHW in the area												3
Don't know or no response												9
4. Has the CHW given you advice on how to grow more nutritious food?[a] **(Tick one)**												
Yes												1
No												2
No CHW in the area												3
Don't know or no response												9

Question no.	*Household sequence no.*	*Specify answer*

1. Respondent

	1	2	3	4	5	6	7	8	9	10	Total	Code
Sequence no. of household in the cluster												
5. Who was consulted the last time any member of the household was ill? **(Tick all who were consulted the last time)**												
No one												0
Private doctor												1
Government facility/Government health centre												2
NGO facility/NGO health centre												3
Traditional healer												4
CHW (community health worker)												5
TBA (traditional birth attendant)												6
Relative												7
Other (*specify overleaf*)												8
Don't know or no response												9
6. Have you or any members of the household participated in any community projects or meetings during the past 3 months?[b] **(Tick one)**												
Yes												1
No												2
Don't know or no response												9
7. What type of water supply is available to the household?[c] **(Tick all answers given)**												
Rainwater container on premises												1
Piped water on premises												2
Well-water on premises												3
Communal tap outside premises												4
Well outside premises												5
Other source (*specify overleaf*)												6
Don't know or no response												9
8. How long does it take you to get to your source of water? **(Tick one)**												
Water is on premises												1
Less than 15 minutes												2
More than 15 minutes												3
Don't know or no response												9

Question no.	Household sequence no.	Specify answer

5. Who was consulted?

7. Water supply

	1	2	3	4	5	6	7	8	9	10	Total	Code
Sequence no. of household in the cluster												
9. What kind of sanitary facilities do you use?[d] (**Tick one**)												
Sewage connection												1
Septic tank for household												2
Pit latrine for household												3
Bucket system for household												4
Neighbour's latrine												5
Communal latrine												6
Wilderness/countryside/fields												7
Other (*specify overleaf*)												8
Don't know or no response												9
10. What methods do you know for preventing malaria? (**Do not prompt**) (**Tick all items mentioned**)												
Bednets												1
Antimalarial drugs given regularly												2
Antimalarial drugs given early												3
Spraying against adult mosquitos												4
Spraying against mosquito larvae												5
Eliminating breeding sites												6
Other (*specify overleaf*)												7
Don't know or no response												9
11. From whom did you get knowledge or information about malaria?[e,f] (**Tick all answers given**)												
Health staff												1
CHW												2
TBA												3
Relatives or neighbours												4
Mass media (e.g., radio)												5
Other (*specify overleaf*)												6
Nobody												7
Don't know or no response												9

Question no.	Household sequence no.	Specify answer
9. Sanitation		
10. Antimalaria methods		
11. Malaria knowledge		

	1	2	3	4	5	6	7	8	9	10	Total	Code
Sequence no. of household in the cluster												
12. Are there any children less than 5 years old living in the household now? **(Tick one)**												
Yes												1
No												2
Don't know or no response												9
(If no, or don't know or no response, draw a line down the column until you get to Q. 21)												
13. When one of your children has diarrhoea, what do you do about giving the child fluids?[g] **(Tick one)**												
Stop giving fluids												1
Decrease amount of fluids												2
Increase amount of fluids												3
Don't change amount												4
Don't know or no response												9
14. Are there any children less than 3 years old living in the household now? **(Tick one)**												
Yes												1
No												2
Don't know or no response												9
(If no, or don't know or no response, draw a line down the column until you get to Q. 21)												
15. Please show me the growth chart of the youngest child less than 3 years old.[h] **(Tick one)**												
Growth chart seen												1
Growth chart not seen												2
(If growth chart not seen, draw a line down the column until you get to Q. 17)												

	1	2	3	4	5	6	7	8	9	10	Total	Code
Sequence no. of household in the cluster												
16. If growth chart is available, does it show that the child has been weighed 3 times or more in the last 12 months?[i] (**Tick one**)												
Yes												1
No, child less than 1 year old												2
No, child more than 1 year old												3
17. Are there any children less than 2 years old living in the household now? (**Tick one**)												
Yes												1
No												2
Don't know or no response												9
(**If no, or don't know or no response, or if respondent is not the mother, draw a line down the column until you get to Q. 21**)												
18. Who examined you during your pregnancy with the youngest child? (**Tick all answers given**)[j]												
Doctor												1
Nurse or midwife												2
Traditional birth attendant[k]												3
Traditional healer												4
Other (*specify opposite*)												5
Nobody												6
Don't know or no response												9
19. Where was your youngest child born? (**Tick one**)												
Hospital												1
Health centre												2
Home, assisted by midwife												3
Home, assisted by TBA[k]												4
Other (*specify opposite*)												5
Don't know or no response												9

Question no.	*Household sequence no.*	*Specify answer*
18. Prenatal care		By whom?
19. Delivery		Where? By whom?

	1	2	3	4	5	6	7	8	9	10	Total	Code
Sequence no. of household in the cluster												
20. What was the weight of your youngest child at birth? (**Tick one**)												
Under 2500 g												1
2500 g or more												2
Not weighed												3
Don't know or no response												9
21. How many girls (aged 7, 8, 9, 10, 11, or 12 years) are living in the household now? (**Tick one**)												
None												0
1												1
2												2
3												3
4												4
5												5
6												6
7												7
More than 7												8
Don't know or no response												9
(**If none, or don't know or no response, draw a line down the column until you get to Q. 23**)												
22. How many of these girls (aged 7, 8, 9, 10, 11, or 12 years) go to school now? (**Tick one**)												
None												0
1												1
2												2
3												3
4												4
5												5
6												6
7												7
More than 7												8
Don't know or no response												9

	1	2	3	4	5	6	7	8	9	10	Total	Code
Sequence no. of household in the cluster												
23. Is the respondent the mother or the male head of household? **(Tick one)**												
Mother												1
Male head of household												2
Other												3
(If other, draw a line down the column until the end of the form)												
24. Are you or your spouse now using a method of child spacing?[l] **(This question is sensitive and may need to be asked in private) (Tick one)**												
Pill												1
IUD												2
Condom												3
Sterilization												4
Other (*specify overleaf*)												5
Not using anything												6
No response												9
25. Who owns this house?[m] **(Tick one)**												
The family												1
A relative												2
Other												3
Don't know or no response												9
26. Can you read this? **(Show specific piece of text) (Tick one)**												
Yes												1
No												2
No response												9

Name of person completing form . . . .

Question no.	*Household sequence no.*	*Specify answer*

24. Child spacing

Notes

a   Use this question only when there is a programme for providing information to households on the particular subject. Similar questions may be asked about the community development worker or agricultural extension worker, if there is one in the area.

b   Further questions may be asked on who participated, the type of meeting, relevance to national or local planning cycle, and specific programmes to be undertaken. For example, this question might be asked about meetings of women's groups, community cleanliness, or immunization campaigns, etc.

c   Categories to be listed here depend on the types and terms used in each country and the specific water supply programmes being undertaken.

d   The categories listed here should reflect the types of sanitary arrangements commonly found or being promoted in the survey areas.

e   Similar questions may be asked about sources of information on other health problems, such as diarrhoea.

f   Similar questions may be asked about acute respiratory infections, etc.

g   Questions about knowledge, attitudes, and practices may also be asked about other targets of health education programmes.

h   Questions may also be asked that probe the mother's understanding of the growth chart, or how the child's upper-arm circumference or weight can be measured directly.

i   The number of weighings and the time period specified in this question should reflect the standards or expected practices in the country.

j   The categories of personnel listed here should reflect the level of detail required in relation to the expected pattern of delivery of prenatal care.

k   It may be possible to determine whether the TBA was trained or untrained by asking for the name of the TBA to be recorded on the back of the page, and checking the names and locations against the list of TBAs trained by the health services in the area.

l   The list of methods should be adapted to the methods currently being promoted. Sensitive questions like this should always be left to the end of the questionnaire.

m   This question is meant to produce information about socioeconomic status. It should be framed according to local conditions and, therefore, instead of being a question about home ownership, it could be about type of house construction, number of rooms, ownership of radio or television, land ownership, income, education, etc., as appropriate.

Form B: Immunization coverage questionnaire

Number of cluster _____   Name of village _____

Date _____   Name of district ——————

		NAME OF CHILD											
Range of birth dates for children aged 12–23 months at time of survey From: _____ To: _____													
Household number from Form A													
Birth date (month/year)													TOTAL
Immunization card	Yes												
	No												
DPT 1	Date/Yes/No												
	Source*												
DPT 2	Date/Yes/No												
	Source												
DPT 3	Date/Yes/No												
	Source												
POLIO 1	Date/Yes/No												
	Source												
POLIO 2	Date/Yes/No												
	Source												
POLIO 3	Date/Yes/No												
	Source												
MEASLES	Date/Yes/No												
	Source												
BCG	Date/Yes/No												
	Scar/Yes/No												
	Source												

* Source (place of immunization): hospital = HOS; health centre = HC; outreach = OUT; nongovernment/private = PRV.

Household number from Form A													
M O T H E R	TT 1	Date/Yes/No											
		Source											
	TT 2 or booster	Date/Yes/No											
		Source											

Reasons for immunization failure

Note: Ask only one question: e.g., "Why was the child not immunized?" or "Why was the child not fully immunized?"

Tick (✓) only the one most relevant reason, according to your judgement. If more than one reason per column is ticked, the results cannot be analysed.

	Household number from Form A											TOTAL
	Immunization status	Fully immunized										
		Partially immunized										
		Not immunized										
Lack of information	1. Unaware of need for immunization											
	2. Unaware of need to return for 2nd or 3rd dose											
	3. Place and/or time of immunization unknown											
	4. Fear of side-reactions											
	5. Wrong ideas about contraindications											
	6.											
Lack of motivation	7. Postponed till another time											
	8. No faith in immunization											
	9. Rumours											
	10.											

Obstacles	11. Place of immunization too far to go													
	12. Time of immunization inconvenient													
	13. Vaccinator absent													
	14. Vaccine not available													
	15. Mother too busy													
	16. Family problem (including illness of mother)													
	17. Child ill—not brought													
	18. Child ill—brought but not immunized													
	19. Long waiting time													
	20.													

Name of person completing form.. .

Guidelines for analysis of results of household questionnaires

Summarizing results per cluster

Immediately after finalizing all the household interviews within a cluster, the members of the survey team should calculate the totals for that cluster, i.e., the number of ticks on each line of the form (covering a maximum of 10 households). This number should be entered in the last column (see Example 1 on page 217).

For clusters that include more than 10 households, the totals in the last column are in fact subtotals. A blank questionnaire can be used for calculating the real totals, by putting the subtotals in the columns (originally meant for ticks) so that they can easily be added up to arrive at the totals for the cluster (see Example 2 on page 218).

Summarizing results per district/region/country

Since, in the final analysis, results will have to be analysed according to district, region, or country, depending on the sample design, they

Example 1

HOUSEHOLD QUESTIONNAIRE

Number of cluster ___*1*___
Date _____

Name of village *aaaaa*
Name of district *bbbbb* *

	1	2	3	4	5	6	7	8	9	10	Total	Code
Sequence no. of household in the cluster	1	2	3	4	5	6	7	8	9	10		
1. Respondent (**Tick one**) (**The mother should always be the respondent if possible**)												
Mother	✓	✓		✓		✓	✓	✓	✓		7	1
Other (*specify overleaf*)			✓		✓					✓	3	2
2. Has the household been visited by a CHW within the last 4 weeks? (**Tick one**)												
Yes	✓					✓	✓	✓			4	1
No		✓	✓								2	2
No CHW in the area				✓					✓		2	3
Don't know or no response					✓					✓	2	9
3. Has the CHW given you advice on sanitation or cleanliness?[a] (Tick one)												
Yes	✓							✓			2	1
No		✓	✓			✓	✓				4	2
No CHW in the area				✓					✓		2	3
Don't know or no response					✓					✓	2	9
4. Has the CHW given you advice on how to grow more nutritious food?[a] (**Tick one**)												
Yes	✓										1	1
No		✓	✓			✓	✓	✓			5	2
No CHW in the area				✓					✓		2	3
Don't know or no response					✓					✓	2	9

* Fictitious district *bbbbb* has 6 clusters of 30 households each.

Example 2

Summary of household questionnaire per cluster*

Number of cluster ___1___   Name of village _aaaaa_
Date _____   Name of district _bbbbb_

	1	2	3	4	5	6	7	8	9	10	Total	Code
Sequence no. of household in the cluster**	1–10	11–20	21–30	x	x	x	x	x	x	x		
1. Respondent (**Tick one**) (**The mother should always be the respondent if possible**)												
Mother	7	7	9								23	1
Other (*specify overleaf*)	3	3	1								7	2
2. Has the household been visited by a CHW within the last 4 weeks? (**Tick one**)												
Yes	4	5	6								15	1
No	2	3	2								7	2
No CHW in the area	2	1	1								4	3
Don't know or no response	2	1	1								4	9
3. Has the CHW given you advice on sanitation or cleanliness?[a] (**Tick one**)												
Yes	2	4	5								11	1
No	4	4	3								11	2
No CHW in the area	2	1	1								4	3
Don't know or no response	2	1	1								4	9
4. Has the CHW given you advice on how to grow more nutritious food?[a] (**Tick one**)												
Yes	1	3	4								8	1
No	5	5	4								14	2
No CHW in the area	2	1	1								4	3
Don't know or no response	2	1	1								4	9

* The original household questionnaire may be used in this way to tabulate totals for clusters of more than 10 households. In this example, there are 30 households in the cluster.
** Put in each column the subtotals as noted in the last column of the original household questionnaire used during the interviews in the cluster. (Column 1 in this example shows the total for households 1–10 from Example 1.)

have to be summarized further. The procedure described for cluster results can also be used for the subsequent steps. Great care should be taken to indicate clearly, on the questionnaires used for summarizing results, the levels and geographical areas to which they apply, and what the columns and the totals represent (see Example 3 on page 220).

Analysing results

When analysing the results, the procedure to be followed is the same, regardless of whether the results are for a district, region, or country. Where a stratified sample design has been used (i.e., sets of clusters sampled to obtain separate estimates for different regions, or for urban versus rural areas) an additional step will be required to compare the results from the various strata, but the procedure described below will be the same for each.

In order to facilitate analysis, an analysis format should be planned in advance, indicating the following items, at least, for each question:

(a) Question number and question itself.
(b) Whether branching or not ("branching": when response is "x", go to question number "y"). Indicate if question is starting point of nested questions.
(c) Number of alternative responses:
    — single ("tick one"),
    — multiple ("tick all that apply").
(d) Range of acceptable responses, and meaning of codes (if coding is used).
(e) What should be tabulated, e.g.:
    — information is for identification only, and need not be tabulated,
    — yes/no/don't know or no response,
    — other frequency distribution,
    — %/average/rate,
    — numbers for use in calculations (denominator or numerator data? From which other questions are data needed for the calculations?).

For the questions on Form A, an analysis format might appear as follows:

Question 1
(a) Respondent?
(b) No branching.

Example 3

Summary of household questionnaire per district*

Number of cluster *1-6*

Date _____

Name of village ___

Name of district *bbbbb*

	1	2	3	4	5	6	7	8	9	10	Total	Code
Sequence no. of cluster**	1	2	3	4	5	6						
1. Respondent (**Tick one**) (**The mother should always be the respondent if possible**)												
Mother	23	21	18	15	24	12					113	1
Other (*specify overleaf*)	7	9	12	15	6	18					67	2
2. Has the household been visited by a CHW within the last 4 weeks? (**Tick one**)												
Yes	15	12	24	9	12	15					87	1
No	7	6	6	9	9	12					49	2
No CHW in the area	4	6	–	–	3	–					13	3
Don't know or no response	4	6	–	12	6	3					31	9
3. Has the CHW given you advice on sanitation or cleanliness?[a] (Tick one)												
Yes	11	6	21	9	6	6					59	1
No	11	12	9	9	15	21					77	2
No CHW in the area	4	6	–	–	3	–					13	3
Don't know or no response	4	6	–	12	6	3					31	9
4. Has the CHW given you advice on how to grow more nutritious food?[a] (**Tick one**)												
Yes	8	3	21	15	9	6					62	1
No	14	15	9	–	12	21					71	2
No CHW in the area	4	6	–	–	3	–					13	3
Don't know or no response	4	6	–	15	6	3					34	9

* In the same way a summary form may be produced per province/region, etc.

** Put in each column the totals from the summaries of household questionnaires per cluster. (Column 1 in this example shows the total for cluster 1 from Example 2.)

(*c*) Single response.
(*d*) Codes: 1 = mother
        2 = other (specify).
(*e*) Tabulate % mothers (might need to tabulate "other" by type if % mothers is relatively low). Might use response to cross-check non-responses to questions 18–20, and for cross-tabulation against 24 and 26.

Question 2
(*a*) Household visited by CHW within the last 4 weeks?
(*b*) No branching.
(*c*) Single response.
(*d*) Codes: 1 = yes
        2 = no
        3 = no CHW in area
        9 = don't know or no response.
(*e*) Tabulate frequency distribution of responses.

Questions 3 and 4: similar to question 2.

Question 5
(*a*) Who was consulted the last time any member of the household was ill?
(*b*) No branching.
(*c*) Multiple response.
(*d*) Codes: 0 = No one
        1 = Private doctor
        2 = Government facility/Government health centre
        3 = NGO facility/NGO health centre
        4 = Traditional healer
        5 = CHW
        6 = TBA
        7 = Relative
        8 = Other (specify)
        9 = Don't know or no response.
(*e*) Tabulate the proportion of each response to the total number of households. (If necessary hand-tabulate "others".)

If it is important to analyse different combinations, more complex coding schemes will be required for analysis and tabulation, starting with the initial tabulation of household results. In general, this is not recommended.

Question 6: similar to question 2.

Question 7
(a) What type of water supply is available to the household?
(b) No branching.
(c) Multiple response.
(d) Codes: 1 = Rainwater container on premises
        2 = Piped water on premises
        3 = Well-water on premises
        4 = Communal tap outside premises
        5 = Well outside premises
        6 = Other source (specify)
        9 = Don't know or no response.
(e) Tabulate the proportion of each response to the total number of households. (If necessary, hand-tabulate any "other sources".)

Question 8: similar to question 2.

Question 9: similar to question 6.

Question 10: similar to question 5.

Question 11: similar to question 7.

Question 12
(a) Are there any children less than 5 years old living in the household now?
(b) Branching question; starting point of nested questions: if "no" or "don't know" or "no response", go to question 21.
(c) Single response.
(d) Codes: 1 = yes
        2 = no
        9 = don't know or no response.
(e) Tabulate proportion of households in which children under 5 years of age are present (total number "yes" divided by total number of households).

Use number of households with children under 5 years of age (total number of "yes") as denominator for question 13.

Question 13
(a) When one of your children has diarrhoea, what do you do about giving the child fluids?
(b) No branching (end of branch).
(c) Single response.

(*d*) Codes: 1 = stop giving fluids
           2 = decrease amount
           3 = increase amount
           4 = don't change amount
           9 = don't know or no response.

(*e*) Tabulate frequency distribution of responses as proportion of households with children under 5 years of age (= total number "yes" in question 12).

Question 14
(*a*) Are there any children less than 3 years old living in the household now?
(*b*) Branching question; starting point of nested questions: if "no" or "don't know" or "no response", go to question 21.
(*c*) Single response.
(*d*) Codes: 1 = yes
           2 = no
           9 = don't know or no response.
(*e*) Tabulate proportion of households with children under 3 years old.

Use number of households with children under 3 years old ("yes") as denominator for question 15.

Question 15: similar to question 13 (however, branching question).

Question 16
(*a*) If the growth chart is available, does it show that the child has been weighed 3 times or more in the last 12 months?
(*b*) No branching (end of branch).
(*c*) Single response.
(*d*) Codes: 1 = yes
           2 = no, child less than 1 year old
           3 = no, child more than 1 year old.
(*e*) Tabulate proportion of children weighed (code 1) in relation to total responses coded 1 and 3 (excluding children of less than 1 year of age from analysis).

Question 17: similar to question 14.

Use number of households with children under 2 years old as denominator for questions 18, 19, and 20.

Questions 18, 19, 20: Tabulate frequency distribution as proportion of households with children under 2 years old.

Question 21

(a) How many girls aged 7, 8, 9, 10, 11, or 12 years are living in the household now?

(b) Branching question: if "none" or "don't know" or "no response", go to question 23.

(c) Single response.

(d) Codes: 0 = none

1 = 1 girl	6 = 6 girls
2 = 2 girls	7 = 7 girls
3 = 3 girls	8 = more than 7 girls
4 = 4 girls	9 = don't know or no response.
5 = 5 girls	

(e) Tabulate total number of girls in the indicated age group (by using the following working table).

Do not take into consideration the number of times codes 0 and 9 are given (i.e., "no girls" or an "unknown" number in indicated age group).

Code (= number of girls in age group) (a)	Total number of times response given (b)	Calculate: (a) × (b)
1		
2		
3		
4		
5		
6		
7		
8*		
Total		_____

The total represents the number of girls in the indicated age group in the households in the sample.

Use total number as denominator for question 22.

*Note that code 8 stands for "more than 7 girls"; the calculation as given above will be an underestimate of the actual number if there are any households with more than 7 girls in this age group in the sample.

Question 22

(a) How many of these girls aged 7, 8, 9, 10, 11, or 12 years old go to school now?

(b) No branching (end of branch).

(c)   Single response.
(d)   Codes: as in question 21.
(e)   Tabulate total number of girls going to school as done for
      question 21.
      Calculate proportion of girls in the age group 7–12 years going to
      school as follows: Total found in question 22 divided by total
      found in question 21.

Question 23: similar to question 12.

Compare with response to question 1 for internal consistency
of interviewers. Might use for cross-tabulation against questions 24
and 26.

Question 24: similar to question 13.

Tabulate responses separately for male heads of household and
mothers (question 23).

Question 25: similar to question 2.

Question 26: similar to question 17.

Final comments

With the help of the above analysis format and a simple pocket
calculator, all the necessary tabulations can be done. This can be
illustrated with some of the figures given in Example 3 (which represents the first page of the summary format for district *bbbbb*, covering
6 clusters with 30 households in each).

- Total number of households in the sample = 180.
- Of all respondents 113/180 = 63% were mothers.
- 87/180 = 48% of the households were visited by the community
  health worker in the past 4 weeks.
- 13/180 = 7% of the households indicated that there is no CHW in
  the area.
  etc.

While the calculations themselves should not be presented in the report, the following type of table (summarizing the outcome of question 5) is very useful:

Person/facility consulted last time any member of the household was ill
(as proportion of households)

District	No one	Private doctor	Govern- ment facility	NGO facility	Tradi- tional healer	CHW	TBA	Rela- ive	Other
bbbbb	7%	35%	27%	2%	2%	10%	7%	15%	3%
ccccc	..	..	..	..	..	..	..	..	..
ddddd	..	..	..	..	..	..	..	..	..
etc.									